M000297952

At The Cross

Noemi Singh

Trilogy Christian Publishers

A Wholly Owned Subsidary of Trinity Broadcasting Network

2442 Michelle Drive

Tustin, CA 92780

Copyright © 2020 by Noemi Singh

All Scripture quotations, unless otherwise noted, taken from THE HOLY BIBLE, NEW INTERNATIONAL VERSION®, NIV® Copyright © 1973, 1978, 1984, 2011 by Biblica, Inc.® Used by permission. All rights reserved worldwide.

Scripture quotations marked (KJV) taken from The Holy Bible, King James Version. Cambridge Edition: 1769.

All rights reserved, including the right to reproduce this book or portions thereof in any form whatsoever.

For information, address Trilogy Christian Publishing

Rights Department, 2442 Michelle Drive, Tustin, Ca 92780.

Trilogy Christian Publishing/ TBN and colophon are trademarks of Trinity Broadcasting Network.

For information about special discounts for bulk purchases, please contact Trilogy Christian Publishing.

Manufactured in the United States of America

Trilogy Disclaimer: The views and content expressed in this book are those of the author and may not necessarily reflect the views and doctrine of Trilogy Christian Publishing or the Trinity Broadcasting Network.

10 9 8 7 6 5 4 3 2 1

Library of Congress Cataloging-in-Publication Data is available.

B-ISBN#: 978-1-64088-931-6

E-ISBN#: 978-1-64088-932-3

I dedicate this writing to my dad, Armando Arrieta. Thank you for always believing in me. I know you're smiling down from heaven. Love you, Dad!

Contents

A Note from the Author

The following characters and their stories are based from biblical Scripture. I have added and embellished their stories to give the reader a better understanding that the people in the Bible had needs and desires very much like ours of today. I hope you will enjoy reading about these women as much as I enjoyed writing about them.

Acknowledgements

First of all, I give glory to God for every good and perfect gift that He has given to me. I'd like to thank my husband, Jonathan Singh, for always encouraging me to never give up on my dream. Thank you to everyone who prayed and believed that this work could be accomplished.

Part 1

He Can Turn It Around

Chapter 1

She could feel the evening chill through her thin garment as she hurried along the streets of Jerusalem. She looked up to see storm clouds gathering in the dark sky. It was late in the afternoon, and her husband, Samuel, would be home soon. She felt a nervous knot in her stomach as she thought of Samuel arriving home before she returned, but it was important for her to get to the marketplace. She had to see Benjamin.

Samuel was an angry man with no patience for others' faults. His anger frightened her, yet she continued hurrying down the street. Samuel was older than she, closer in age to her own father. After Samuel's first wife died, her father had arranged for their marriage. Her father and Samuel were close friends and both were well-respected religious leaders of the synagogue.

Initially, she had been happy to be Samuel's wife. He was a powerful, intelligent man, and she had been proud to be his wife. She would dream of the day that they would have children of their own, but whenever she broached the subject with Samuel, he would laugh at her and say, how could she take care of children when she was a child herself? She tried to make their home a loving, comfortable home, but it seemed that no matter what she did, he was always angry with her. He would often say she was ignorant and unworthy to be his wife. He told her that he regretted marrying her because of her foolishness. She would cry and plead with him to forgive her whenever she infuriated him, but he would walk away and ignore her tears. Frequently, he would threaten to divorce her for being such a horrible wife. She would cry and beg him not to do that, but he would laugh and walk away. One day she quietly followed him as he left their house and saw him enter the home of a well-known prostitute. She couldn't believe what she was seeing. It felt like the wind had been knocked out of her. He stayed inside the

11

house for about thirty minutes and then left. She was heartbroken, she felt ugly and worthless. She confronted him that evening when he returned home. She asked him why he went to another woman when he had a wife at home who loved him. He slapped her and told her to shut up. He said that she had no right to follow him and that she was an insecure, jealous woman. Something inside of her changed after that. Finally, after being rejected for so long, she stopped believing in their marriage. Her heart had been hurt and broken so many times that she finally stopped feeling anything. Until the day that she met Benjamin.

Benjamin was her lover. They had been lovers for several months. She had met him in the marketplace where he sold pottery. She remembered the day distinctly when their eyes met and he smiled at her. He approached her and said, "How can such a beautiful woman look so sad?"

After that, she was caught in a web of deceit and perverseness. She visited the marketplace frequently, and he would step away so that they could talk and get to know one another. He always complimented her and often gave her small gifts to show her that he had been thinking of her. She was flattered by his attention, and like a dry dessert place after a storm, she soaked up the attention that she craved. At first, they talked of silly things, but later she began to confide in him and tell him of the horrible things that Samuel said to her. He would listen patiently and dry her tears from her face. He wanted to confront Samuel and make him stop hurting her, but she would beg him not to say anything. As time went on, one thing led to another; and soon she found herself in the comfort of his arms. She knew that what she was doing was wrong. If anyone ever found out, they both would be stoned to death, but she couldn't help herself. Only when she was with Benjamin did she feel happy and loved. Unlike Samuel, he made her feel pretty and cared for. He said he loved her and wanted to spend the rest of his life with her.

Chapter 1

They dreamed and planned how someday they would marry and live together forever.

Now as she approached the market-place, she quickly went over to Benjamin's place of business. He looked up and smiled when he saw her and immediately walked towards the back where she met up with him. They went upstairs to Benjamin's room where they often met. He drew her into his arms while she attempted to explain to him that she didn't have much time, but he began kissing her. She soon forgot about Samuel and focused totally on Benjamin. After a while, she lay in his arms, enjoying the moment of intimacy. As they lay in his bed talking softly and planning how they would run away together then the door to his room suddenly burst open—and there stood Samuel.

Chapter 2

Never had she seen Samuel look so horrifying. He stood at the door, breathing heavy with a fierce look on his face, and both hands clenched into a fist. She flew off the bed and grabbed her garment around her. He came towards her, grabbing her by the neck and throwing her to the ground. She began crying and pleading with him not to hurt her, but he said nothing. He was like a crazed animal. As she lay on the ground, he began kicking her. Then he pulled her up by her hair and slapped her across the face. Her nose began to bleed, and her face swelled up. He picked her up and thrust her against the wall. He cursed and screamed at her. She turned to Benjamin for help, but he was crouched in a corner whimpering. Samuel pulled her up by her hair and said, "Look at your lover. He cries like a girl." He laughed, and then he dragged her out of the room, down the stairs, and up the street like an animal.

Great drops of rain had started to fall as Samuel dragged her through the city streets. She was humiliated and terrified, but more than anything, she was disappointed. Benjamin had let her down. She always knew that Samuel hated her, but she thought that Benjamin would have cared. Why didn't he protect her? She knew that once her father found out about this incident, he would disown her from the family. She had to face her sentence all alone and more than likely Samuel would probably have her put to death.

Samuel took her to the temple where she would be judged. But when he arrived, there was a crowd inside, listening to that *blasphemer* Jesus teach from the Scriptures. He pulled her toward the back and found the chief priest pacing the room. Her father stood off to the side, an angry look of disapproval on his face. Samuel threw her at the chief priest's feet and said, "I found her in the act of adultery. I want divorce papers, and I want her put to death."

Her father scowled and looked down on her with contempt. The chief priest stopped and looked at the woman. He stayed quiet for several minutes and then pulled Samuel and her father off to the side.

"Samuel, I have an idea. Why don't we take her to Jesus and let him decide? If he has her put to death, he will lose credibility with the people. If he lets her go, he will break the law. Either way, he will be discredited."

Samuel pondered this idea for several minutes and then reluctantly agreed to allow Jesus to judge his wife. "Very well, but I still want the letter of divorce," he replied.

"Of course," the chief priest responded. He then had some of the Pharisees and scribes take her to Jesus.

Chapter 3

As Samuel, her father, and the chief priest led the way towards Jesus, the Pharisees and scribes pushed her forward, kicking her whenever she lost her footing. Her garment was torn, and her face was bruised and swollen. She knew she was going to die. The room became quiet as the group entered the area where Jesus was teaching.

She knew how much Samuel and the other religious leaders hated Jesus. There were many nights that Samuel would come home ranting and raving of how this man Jesus was deceiving the people. He claimed that Jesus was using witchcraft to perform the miracles that everyone was talking about. He and the other leaders, including her father, were determined to expose his deceptions and prove to the people that they were following a counterfeit miracle worker. Samuel was livid that Jesus could recite the Scriptures word-for-word and yet would sit down to eat with tax collectors. Samuel claimed that the day would come when they would be able to ensnare this self-proclaimed prophet and put an end to all this nonsense.

But the young woman had also heard from some of the other women how this man Jesus went around the region performing acts of goodness. How he spoke of love and forgiveness. She had heard of the wonderful miracles he performed. He gave sight to the blind and healed the lepers. One day she had been invited by some of the women from town to go out to the wilderness to hear his teachings and to see the signs and wonders, but when Samuel found out, he locked her in the house and forbade her to go. He threatened that he would destroy her if he found out that she had gone with the women. She had stayed home that day, locked in her house, hoping that he would calm down by the time he returned home that evening.

Now as they approached Jesus, he stopped speaking and turned to look at them as they entered the temple. His eyes were full of compassion as he looked at the young woman. She dropped her head in shame, afraid of seeing her reflection in his eyes. Conviction swept over her as she stood before him. Ashamed for what she had done, she felt dirty as she stood with her head bowed. She knew that everyone was looking at her, judging her for her sins. She never thought that she would be marked as an adulteress, but somehow the circumstances of her life and the bad choices she had made led her to this point. Now she stood before Jesus, her fate in the hands of this man. Even though she had heard many wonderful things about him, she knew she deserved to die. There was no question about it; she had been caught in the act of her sin. Then the scribes and Pharisees said to Jesus, "Teacher, this woman was caught in adultery, in the very act. Now Moses, in the law, commanded us that such should be stoned. But what do you say?"

Surprisingly, he didn't say anything but stooped down and wrote on the ground with his finger, as though he did not hear. No one noticed what he was writing, so they continued to question him; and finally he looked up and said to them, "He who is without sin among you, let him throw a stone at her first."

He then bent over and continued to write on the ground. That's when she noticed what he was writing. He was writing the names of her accusers, including Samuel and her father with dates of when they had visited the city's prostitutes. The others must have become aware of what he was writing because one by one, they began exiting the room. Then Jesus stood up and looked around. He said to the woman, "Where are your accusers? Has no one condemned you?"

She answered, "No one, Lord."

Then he said to her, "Neither do I condemn you. Go and sin no more."

"You mean, I am free to go?" she asked.

He smiled, nodded at her, and turned to resume his teaching. She turned to walk away, sobbing and grateful for his mercy toward her. Why would he forgive her? She wondered. Everyone else had abandoned her, and yet he had protected her. Suddenly, she felt a gentle arm around her shoulders; she turned and saw an older woman with kind eyes and a warm smile next to her.

"Hello, my name is Mary Magdalene," she said. "Do you have a place to go?" she asked.

The young woman was stunned. Why were these people being so nice to her? She shook her head *no*. She hadn't even thought about where she would go.

Mary Magdalene smiled and asked, "Would you like to come home with me? I would love the company!"

All she could do was nod her head *yes*. Tears streamed down her face as she followed Mary Magdalene home.

Chapter 4

As they walked to Mary Magdalene's home, a light drizzle fell upon them. The streets were empty, and the water from the rain gave everything a fresh, clean look. When they arrived at Mary Magdalene's house, the young woman immediately sensed a sweet peace in her home. It was a comfortable home, warm and inviting for the young woman. Mary Magdalene brought out a fresh garment for her to change into and put out a basin with water for her to wash her wounds. The whole time Mary Magdalene worked, she spoke softly to the young woman, making her feel comfortable and secure. Once the young woman was done changing clothes and washing up, she came out to find that Mary Magdalene had hot soup and warm bread waiting for her.

The meal was delicious, and as she ate her food, Mary Magdalene explained to her that she was the owner of a small business that sold cloth. She went on to say that if the young woman was interested, she could work for her. She offered her room and board plus a small income to meet any other needs she might have. The young woman sat there quietly as she listened to Mary Magdalene's soft voice. She finally picked up her head and asked, "Why are you doing this? I was caught in the act of adultery. I am a sinful woman."

Mary Magdalene smiled and said, "Let me tell you a story of a woman who had done so much evil that seven devils tormented her. She was an angry woman full of bitterness and hate. She offered herself to men so that she could control and use them for her own benefit. Until the day that she became deathly sick. A friend of hers told her of a 'miracle worker' named Jesus who could cure her. She went to where Jesus was and listened to his teachings. While he spoke, a powerful presence came upon her, and she fell to the ground, trembling and jerking violently. Jesus immediately approached her and commanded the devils to leave her. She lay there exhausted, unable to move for several minutes. When she got up, she was healed and felt like a new woman. I was that woman," Mary Magdalene explained. "Jesus set me free. Since then, I have been serving and loving him. He had mercy on me and forgave me of my sins; just like he did for you."

The young woman sat there listening to this remarkable woman and her story. It was hard to imagine this warm, kind person had once done such horrible things, but she understood how a person could get involved in something without realizing it, until it was too late. She also understood that there was something about Jesus and his forgiveness that changed a person.

They sat up most of the night talking. Mary Magdalene answered her questions regarding Jesus and what he had done for her. She was a wise and compassionate woman who cared and wanted to help the young woman. As the night wore on, their eyes grew weary, and they both began trying to stifle their yawns. Finally, Mary Magdalene stood up and said that they should go to bed, there was plenty of time to talk tomorrow. "That is, if you agree to take me up on my offer to stay and work for me?" she asked with a twinkle in her eye.

The young woman smiled and said, "I would be honored to work for you."

"Wonderful!" Mary Magdalene responded. "We are going to have a great time together. I just know it."

Chapter 5

From that night on, her life changed. She knew that Jesus had forgiven her but even more than that he had given her something that she never had before—acceptance. Because of that, she no longer felt fear. He had turned an impossible situation into something wonderful. Just knowing that Jesus loved her and accepted her gave her a confidence and strength she never experienced. She knew that Samuel probably still wanted her dead, but she felt peace knowing that God would protect her, and she was smart enough not to go near the temple where he congregated. Something else too, she no longer needed Benjamin. It was as though he never existed in her life. It was strange to think that just a few days prior, she had been obsessed with him. Now she never thought of him. She was able to enjoy her life feeling a sense of accomplishment at the end of each day. In the evenings, Mary Magdalene would share with her the experiences she had since knowing Jesus. They would sit and worship the Lord with hands raised and tears flowing freely. A wonderful presence would fill their hearts and minds. Whenever Jesus was in Jerusalem, neither one of them missed the opportunity to go and hear him teach and minister to the crowds.

There were days Mary Magdalene would leave her in control of the business while she followed Jesus and the others to minister to those in need.

On those days, the young woman worked hard to run a smooth business, grateful for the opportunity that Mary Magdalene offered her. All these miracles on a daily basis, yet there was one that stood out above the others.

Mary Magdalene kept her earnings in a small box on the top shelf. Every day she would put in whatever earnings she had made that day; some days there was hardly more than a few coins, yet whenever there was a need to make a purchase or a debt to pay, there was always enough. Mary Magdalene never counted her earnings, yet she always knew there would be enough. The other thing she did was that every day she took out large handfuls of coins to give to the ministry of Jesus. When the young woman asked her about not counting her earnings and always having enough, Mary Magdalene smiled knowingly and responded, "The Lord provides."

Chapter 6

The winter months passed quickly for the young woman. She had learned so much and had become confident and strong. She loved the Lord with all her heart and loved Mary Magdalene like a daughter loves her mother. It was the best time of her life. As spring approached, the colors on the hillside became vibrant with a variety of different wildflowers and rich green grass. Jesus often met with his followers on the hillsides of Jerusalem.

It had become more dangerous for him to enter the city and teach at the temple the way he had previously done because of the religious leaders that were determined to destroy him. The young woman sensed that Samuel and her father were probably two of the men that were plotting some sort of evil device to stop Jesus.

One night, right before the Passover feast, she and Mary Magdalene had already gone to bed, when they were awakened by a loud banging on the door. Mary Magdalene jumped up to open the door with the young woman right behind her. There stood Mary, Jesus' mother, and John, one of his disciples. They both had a frightened look on their face as they began to explain that Jesus had been arrested. They told them that they were on their way to the courtyard where Jesus was being held. Mary Magdalene quickly turned to the young woman.

"Go," the young woman said, "I'll take care of everything here."

So Mary Magdalene quickly grabbed her cloak and went out into the night with John and Mary. She watched them as they hurried along into the darkness. The night was cool, and she shivered, wrapping her garment tightly around herself. Fear gripped her heart. In the pit of her stomach, she knew that Samuel was probably connected to this evil incident. She could still recall the viciousness in his eyes whenever he spoke of Jesus. She slowly closed the door and went back inside the house.

Once inside, she began pacing the small house. She was too anxious to go back to sleep. She tried to do some mending but was unable to concentrate on her task. She left the garment she had been mending and went to the oven to throw in some more wood for a fire. She was terrified, and tears kept clouding her vision. Finally, after several attempts to find something to do, she knelt on the cold floor and began to pray. Tears streamed down her face, and great sobs escaped her lips as she knelt before her God. "Oh, God, I know I am the most unworthy of all to come into your presence. My heart is heavy with pain as I kneel before you. I pray that your will be done on earth as it is in heaven. Give us peace in this dark hour and deliver us from evil. For thine is the kingdom, the power, and the glory. Amen."

She cried for her Lord and what he must be going through. She remembered how he had defended her as she stood before her accusers. Who would defend him now? As she knelt in that room, on that midnight hour, fear gripped her heart. After several hours, she got up from her kneeling position. Nothing seemed to have changed. Where was God? Why did it seem as though he wasn't listening? She had work to do, so she went on with her day, but her mind was not on her work. The burden in her heart was heavy, and tears flowed freely from her eyes throughout the day.

As the day wore on, customers would give her tidbits of information of what was happening at the courtyard. The news was not good. She kept hoping to hear that he had been released, but the news kept getting worse. She prayed to God, throughout the day as customers came and went from the shop.

In the middle of the day, storm clouds began to gather in the sky. The day became dark and cold. She stepped outside as a light drizzle began to fall and heard the people talking as they passed her. They spoke of the events occurring at the courtyard. Someone said that a crucifixion was about to take place, and another said that it was Jesus who was being crucified. Crucified? Why would they crucify Jesus?

He was not a criminal! When she heard the news, she immediately closed down the business and quickly ran down the street towards the place where Jesus was. This could not be happening. This news was more than she could bear. She ran, not noticing the cold air that blew all around her or the throng of people gathered in the streets. She heard yelling and jeering from the violent crowd, but she continued to run. She saw the crowd moving slowly towards the outskirts of the city. She followed the multitude towards a hill called Golgotha.

She climbed the hill with the rest of the crowd. It was a steep, rocky hill, and she occasionally lost her footing, scraping her hands and knees on the stony terrain. She was out of breath when she got to the top of the hill; but she barely noticed, for there, hanging on a cross, was her precious Lord.

Chapter 7

He was disfigured and barely recognizable. His flesh hung from his body like strips of cloth from a torn garment. Blood poured out of his wounds, leaving a large puddle of blood at the foot of the cross. He looked lifeless, and she wondered if he was already dead when suddenly, he said in a loud voice, "Father, forgive them for they know not what they do."

Hearing those words, she fell to her face, crying. Even after all they had done to him, he was still forgiving them. How could anyone do this to her Lord? She thought of how she had foolishly lived, bringing shame to her family, and yet he had forgiven her. Here he was again, forgiving those who deserved to die. As she knelt on the ground, crying, knowing that it was she who deserved to die and not Jesus, she felt a gentle hand on her shoulder. She looked up to see Mary Magdalene with tears running down her face. They hugged and attempted to comfort each other as the sky overhead grew darker. She looked up into the face of Jesus and saw that he was watching her. Even though his body was torn and beaten, his eyes were observant. He must have been in great pain, yet his eyes looked upon her with love. Then suddenly, he spoke out, "It is finished." He then said, "Father, into thy hands, I commit my Spirit." He bowed his head and died.

Large drops of rain began pouring from the dark sky. It was as though creation mourned for the death of Jesus. Thunder roared and flashes of lightening shot across the atmosphere. Many ran for cover, but a small group that loved him stayed behind. She watched as they took his body down from the cross, and John and Mary wrapped him in a white cloth that immediately was stained red from his blood. Mary cried, as she wiped his face and kissed his hair. Some men carried his body to a tomb that had been given to him. She followed Mary and Mary Magdalene as they observed where his body was laid. She knew that Mary would need Mary Magdalene close by, so she left them alone.

She walked through the garden where he was buried. Rain continued to pour down, soaking her garments, but she didn't care. She was grief-stricken, and sorrow filled her heart. Her world was shattered and seemingly beyond repair. She thought of the evil that she had witnessed and knew that this was beyond comprehension. She cried and wondered if she would ever smile or laugh again. She walked without any regard to where she was going. She was the one who deserved to die, and yet they had taken the life of the one who had restored life to her. The day was dark, and the future seemed questionable. There seemed to be no hope left in this world. Then she recalled something that she had heard Jesus say, "The Son of Man must suffer many things and be rejected by the elders and chief priests and scribes, and be killed and be raised the third day."

Was it possible that he would raise himself from the dead on the third day? She began to increase her pace as she walked through the garden contemplating the possibility. Her steps became lighter, and the burden from her heart began to dissipate while a slow smile began to form on her face. She had seen him raise others from the dead, why not raise himself? The rain had stopped, and her clothes began to dry as she continued to recall what Jesus had often said, "Fear not, only believe."

A warm peace came upon her, and she basked in the presence of God, kneeling there in the garden where Jesus often knelt. She heard his voice from within say to her, "With God, nothing is impossible." He gently spoke to her, assuring her of his presence. She was unaware how long she knelt there, allowing the presence of God to fill her mind and heart.

When she finally got up from kneeling, the sun was breaking through the sky. She felt refreshed and calm. Suddenly, the clouds opened up, and a burst of sunshine warmed her face. The air smelled of fresh rain, and the flowers sparkled from the drops of water that still covered their petals. She looked up towards the sky and saw a perfect rainbow, its rich colors filling the fresh, clean sky. It was the sign of God's covenant with man. This was a sign from God that he was faithful to his promises. It was time for her to stop crying and trust God to turn this nightmare into something glorious. She knew that he was the one to turn an impossible situation into a wonderful opportunity. He had done it before, and she knew he would do it again.

Part 2
His Compassions Fail Not

Dawn was just breaking through the darkened sky as the woman stepped out of her small home to breathe in the freshness of the cool morning. The frigid breeze embraced her as she pulled her shawl close around her shoulders to protect her arms from the chill of the morning air. The morning dew glistened on the grass, and the trees swayed in the breeze. And somewhere nearby, a rooster crowed his morning greeting, and birds sang their daybreak salutation; but for the heartbroken woman, her surroundings were meaningless. It had been a difficult night, and she took in deep gulps of air attempting to stifle the sobs that lodged in her heart. Tears streamed down her face as she looked up to the heavens where light was just breaking, and the sky spread out its colors of yellow, pink, and blue and cried out, "Please, God, save my son."

The woman was a widow. Her husband had died several years before leaving her with a small son to bring up alone. It had been difficult to raise him by herself with no one to help with his upkeep, but he was a delightful boy who brought joy and warmth to her cold world. Many times, she would come home after toiling all day at some menial job out in the field, exhausted and weary from the day's turmoil to be greeted by hugs and kisses from her small boy. She enjoyed listening to him as he played outside with his giggles and screams of excitement as he ran through the streets playing games with the other children of the neighborhood. In the evenings, he would sit down next to her in the small house listening intently as she told him the stories of Abraham, Moses, and David. Soon, his small head would lean up against her chest, and his breathing would grow even and steady as he fell off to sleep dreaming of seas opening up and giants being slain. She would carry him to bed and kiss his sweet cheek and lovingly touch his tousled hair, thanking God for this wonderful gift he had given her when he gave her this son. He was her anchor, and she doted on him. As he got older, he was a wonderful hardworking young man, striving to assist his mother in whatever he could. And soon learning a trade as a butcher, he was able to provide a decent home for him and his mother. She was so very proud of this young man and what he was becoming. What more could she ask for? She was a blessed woman until that day that disaster struck.

He had come home one day from his job complaining of a sore throat, cough, and tightness in his chest. He told his mother that he didn't feel well and was going to bed early. She brewed him some tea and gave him a balm of herbs to rub on his chest. He sipped a little of the tea and fell off to sleep. Throughout the night, the cough became more persistent and bloody. By morning, he had a high fever and was barely coherent. She nursed him throughout the day and into the evening. Later that night, she sent one of the neighborhood children to ask her sister, who lived down the road, to come and assist in caring for her son. But as the second night wore on, it was evident that he was not getting better. He was hot to the touch, and the water she tried to give him only dribbled down his chin. She continued to try and soothe his fever with cool, wet towels on his head and pouring drops of water on his cracked, dried lips. The bloody cough continued, and his weak feverish body withered in pain. This went on for several days. Her close friends and neighbors brought dishes of delicious-smelling meals and begged her to eat a little something, but she could not eat. Some of the ladies took shifts to help her nurse her son, but she never left his side. She sat by her son's bedside praying to God for mercy.

It was the morning of the fourth day when she finally went out for a breath of fresh air. She was praying to God for mercy and compassion when suddenly, her sister called her from the open door. "Rebecca, come quick, he's asking for you."

As she ran back into the house, she approached his bed and knelt on the floor to gaze into his face. His eyes were open, and his voice was low and raspy. He looked into her eyes and said, "Mama, I love you, and I'm sorry for leaving you."

She grabbed his hand, but he closed his eyes, took one last breath, and was gone. The others in the room began to wail with grief, but she just stared at him, stunned. She couldn't believe that her precious son was gone. How could this be? It had always been the two of them together. He was her life. She had dreams and plans for him. He was going to get married one day and have children. There was still so much to do. But as she stared at his lifeless face, she suddenly realized that he was gone, and she would never see his wonderful smile again. She would never hear his voice or feel his hugs. She was all alone; this time, for real. She collapsed on the floor in a heap and heard the most sorrowful scream of pain she had ever heard. It sounded like a wounded frightened animal crying and howling in torture. Then suddenly, she realized that the sound was coming from deep within her soul. The others tried to pull her up, but she fought them, struggling to hold her son one last time. Her sister whispered soothing, comforting words into her ear, but she could not hear them. All she knew was that she couldn't let him go. They were going to take him away and prepare him for burial, and she wasn't ready for that. They wanted to dig a hole and put him in the ground forever, and she couldn't allow that to happen. Not yet, give her more time. It was too soon. He was so young. She wasn't prepared to bury her son! But unfortunately, preparations had to be made. And as difficult as it was, the people around her began the sorrowful task. Someone had called for one of the religious leaders, and he began to recite the traditional blessing, "Blessed are you, Lord, our God, King of the universe, the true Judge." He tore his robe, near his heart and began to recite the religious prayers and readings from the Scriptures. Her sister began the task of preparing the ointments needed to cleanse and dress the body. Women came and went into her home bringing the necessary spices and herbs for the purification of the body. Outside in the distance, the sound of a hammer was pounding as someone built the coffin. She sat in her room staring into the distance, not making a sound, not moving a muscle, stiff and paralyzed with grief. Where was God? She had called out to him yet he had not answered her. Why? She had always tried to live a righteous life. She had tried to raise her son in the fear of the Lord. Why had God failed her now? Just a few weeks ago, she and her son had first heard about Jesus, a wonderful teacher and prophet of God whose fame had gone throughout Israel. Everyone was talking about the wonderful words of teaching and the powerful miracles he was performing. Early one morning, she and her son traveled to the countryside to hear this great man and to see for themselves the signs and wonders. He taught that nothing was impossible for God, and they saw him heal the sick, cleanse the lepers, and cast out devils. He proclaimed that he was here to heal the brokenhearted and to forgive sins. His words had penetrated their souls, and they both felt such peace and joy as they left the countryside and returned to their home. But now as she sat in her home with a pain that was indescribable deep in her heart and her son lay lifeless covered in a sheet on a hard-wooden table, she wondered, *Why was God so far away?* If only Jesus had been here, then maybe her son would still be alive. If only she had been able to send for him before her son had died. But he was probably busy preaching and doing miracles in Capernaum, and now it was too late.

As the morning wore on, a crowd began to gather outside of her home. Friends and family began arriving, bringing plates of food. They hugged and cried with her, giving words of comfort and love, but nothing could take away the ache and emptiness from her heart. Everywhere she looked, people gathered in corners whispering together. Many were huddled in groups asking the questions that had yet to be answered. Where would she go? How would she live? Her son had been her source of income. She was too old to go out and work and she had no other children to provide for her. What was to become of this poor widow? Her sister lived down the road, but she was poor and lived in a small home with her husband and five children. Would she be able to take her in too?

Later that afternoon, her sister approached her and said, "Rebecca, it's time." She sorrowfully looked up at her sister and nodded. Slowly, she rose to her feet and approached the table where her son lay. He was dressed in burial clothing. He looked so handsome with his dark hair combed back, his face cleaned, and his beard trimmed. She gently brushed his hair back from his forehead and lovingly touched his cheek. He was still her baby boy, and she was going to miss him terribly. Great tear drops fell from her eyes and landed on her son. She loved him so much, and now he was gone. She laid her head on his chest and cried silently. "Oh, God," she prayed, "please help me. Have mercy on your maidservant and hear my cry."

Gently, her sister pulled her away, so the men could lay her son in the coffin they had made. She stood back as they laid him gently into the coffin, covering him with her prayer shawl. Several men lifted up the coffin and began the procession to the cemetery. The widow and the other women followed slowly out the door, keeping a few steps behind the coffin.

The mood was dark, and the crowd was quiet as they slowly made their way through the city towards the cemetery. The clouds were gray, and the air was damp and heavy. The cold chill penetrated deeper into her heart as the widow cried silently burying her face in her veil. Her sister and neighbor walked beside her, gently holding her and leading her behind the coffin. It was a somber walk as people stood alongside watching the coffin, and the grieving mother walk towards her son's final resting place. Never had she imagined burying her son. She always thought that she would pass away first, yet here she was, following the casket that carried her son. She walked with heavy steps down that dusty road of despair. And with each step she took, it only brought her closer to that final destination where she would have to say goodbye to him. As they approached the gate to the city, the crowd grew larger, and the people began to scramble about. The crowd became noisier and more boisterous, and suddenly the clouds parted and the sun shone through. The warmth of the sun rested on her shoulders, and she looked up to see the brilliant blue of the sky and the brightness of the sun. Raising her hand, she shielded her eyes and squinted with her swollen eyes to see what was causing the commotion in the crowd. That's when she saw a bright light stop in front of her son's coffin. She blinked her eyes, trying to clear and adjust her vision and then there he was Jesus. He stood in the middle of the crowd, not moving but looking at her with such compassion and intensity in his eyes. He was a tall, slim man with brown hair that reached his shoulders. And he carried himself with authority yet with humility that made him approachable. His light-colored eyes penetrated into the depths of her soul seeing the pain and anguish that tormented her heart. A sudden hush came upon the crowd as he quietly walked towards her, and reaching out his hand, he gently touched her shoulder. "Do not weep," he said. Then he approached the coffin and laid his hand on her son and said. "Young man, I say to you, arise."

Immediately, the young man sat up and looked around in confusion, but then his eyes focused on Jesus, and a look of peace came upon him. A small whisper escaped his lips as he said, "I knew you would come."

Jesus turned to the men that were standing with him and asked them to help the young man out of the coffin. When the young man was standing, Jesus smiled broadly and tenderly embraced the young man then immediately turned him over to his mother. The crowd began to gasp and cheer as the son turned and walked towards his mother. The woman looked on in wonder at the amazing scene being played out before her. Suddenly, it seemed as though the sun shone brighter and the colors became more vibrant. A heavy weight lifted from her shoulders, and she stood straighter as she watched her precious son walk towards her with arms reaching out towards her and a smile that extended from ear to ear.

She stood in awe, unable to move and not fully understanding what was happening. Tears streamed down her face, and her heart pounded as her precious son was reached out to her when suddenly, she fell to her knees sobbing the words, "Thank you, Jesus. You are truly the Son of God."

The most amazing miracle had occurred her son was alive! God had answered her prayer, and all she could do was laugh as tears poured down her face while her son scooped her up in his arms.

Two years later

Two years passed since that glorious day when Jesus stepped into her world and rescued her from a life of despair by returning life to her dead son. That first week, they feasted and celebrated with friends and family, proclaiming the wonderful news. The young man told how he had pleaded with God to send Jesus to heal his body and protect his mother. The mother told of the compassion and love Jesus had shown them. It was a time of rejoicing for the wonderful miracle God had given them. From that day forward, whenever Jesus was in their region, they packed up a lunch and followed him to hear his teachings and glory in his presence. The disciples soon knew them by name, and Jesus would often approach them to say hello and give them a hug. The richness of his teachings and seeing the signs and wonders filled their hearts and minds, and they grew in the knowledge and wisdom of God. It was a wonderful time, and the quality of their life changed in every aspect because of the revelation of the Scriptures that Jesus brought to light.

Because of their gratitude towards the Master for the wonderful miracle he had done for them, they contributed to his ministry on a regular basis. The woman always made it a point to give a special offering during the Passover feast because truly, the Lord had passed over them and allowed her son to live just like he had done for the Israelites back in Egypt. So as Passover grew near, she and her son began to prepare for the journey to Jerusalem to celebrate the feast and to give and honor the Lord. It was a three-day journey. So early one morning, they loaded their mule and began the walk to the Holy City. There were many travelers making the same pilgrimage down to the temple, for it was an ancient tradition to celebrate the Passover in the Holy City.

It was a beautiful day as they neared the holy city of Jerusalem. The sun was bright, and the air was crisp. The city sat up on a hill. As they began their ascent up to the city, the air became charged with the excitement as travelers made their way to the city of God. This last part of the journey always made the woman feel so humbled as she climbed the steep road to offer her gratitude to the Almighty for giving her son a second life. He was now married, and they were expecting their first child. Life was perfect, and she owed it all to Jesus!

As they journeyed closer to the city, the atmosphere changed and the woman noticed that people were huddled together whispering and shaking their heads. Some were weeping and many looked solemn and concerned. She approached a woman who was selling fruit at a small stand alongside the road and asked her what was troubling everyone.

The woman told her that Jesus the prophet had been arrested and was sentenced to crucify. He was up on the hill called Golgotha. The woman gasped with dismay and turned to her son and his wife to convey the news she had just heard.

Her son quickly tied his mule to a post and grabbed his wife's and mother's hand and began to hurry up to see for himself the tragic news he had just heard. As they ascended the steep road that led to Golgotha, the crowd grew larger and many were loudly crying and falling to the ground in despair. Some stood in disbelief with tears streaming down their faces.

The woman stumbled a few times as her son hurriedly pulled her up to the hill. The road was rocky, and the crowd was boisterous as they ran to see what lay before them. When they reached the top of the hill, she saw three crosses and Jesus hung on the middle cross. His head was bowed and blood stained his body. Both his hands and feet were pieced with large spikes. His side was torn open, and his flesh was in shreds. His head and hair were blood soaked. It looked like he had been there for several hours because the blood had dried and matted in his hair.

He was unrecognizable, but as they approached, he looked up and made eye contact with them, and then she recognized his eyes—piercing and deep yet full of love and compassion. She fell to the ground, shaking and crying, as her son knelt beside her with his arm around her, attempting to comfort her as he too sobbed in disbelief.

How could this happen? He was a life giver! How could they do this to him? He was the kindest, most loving person she had ever known. He had given her hope and a future after she had lost it all. Now he hung on a cross like a common criminal—disfigured and tortured. Why? How could this happen and why?

Questions and anguish began to consume her mind when suddenly, she felt a peace come upon her. It caressed her like a warm blanket. It was soothing and comforting, and she remembered his words—"I am the resurrection and the life. He who believes in me, though he may die he shall live. And whoever lives and believes in me shall never die."

Was it possible that he could raise himself up from the grave? Yes, of course, it was possible! He had done it for her son. Why couldn't he raise himself up? Suddenly, she knew all was well. She knew that this was a temporal pain, but he would rise up to accomplish the will of Almighty God!

She remembered many times hearing him tell someone who was hurting, "Fear not, only believe." So she stood up from the ground, dusted herself off, held her head up high, and told the Lord, "I am not afraid for I believe."

Suddenly, Jesus called out with a loud voice, "Father, into your hands I commit my spirit." He took a deep breath, and his head bowed down.

He was gone, yet she knew in her heart of hearts that he would be back for nothing was impossible for him. Death would never again scare her for she knew the life giver!

Part 3

She Had No Right

Chapter 8

She was aware of the pounding of her heart, against her ribs, keeping pace with the soft drumming of the rhythmic sound of her feet as she ran through the streets of Sidon. Suddenly, she heard the noise from the crowd before she actually saw them. They were loud, calling out his name, and asking for mercy. She had heard from acquaintances that he was staying at a house in the city. He had come for relaxation, before returning to his ministry in the Jewish region. As she approached the house, where the crowd gathered, she realized that it was going to be difficult for her to get inside. She felt disappointment and despair creep into her heart, but she quickly brushed the feelings aside. Her daughter needed her to succeed in speaking with the Master.

The crowd pressed against the door of the house, and two large, burly men stood at the entrance, guarding the door. The two men were explaining to the crowd that Jesus had come to rest and would not be ministering while he was staying there. The crowd begged and cried, pressing against the men, but the men were adamant in not allowing them inside. She stood at the edges of the crowd trying to press through but with no success. She had to get to Jesus. She could not have come all this way only to return to her daughter with yet more disappointing news. She pleaded with the people around her to help her get close. They only looked at her with scorn and distaste. After all, she was not an Israelite.

In reality, she had no right to be asking anything from Jesus. It was a well-known fact that the Messiah was to come to the Jewish people. Many were convinced that Jesus was their Savior, their long-awaited Messiah. Yet the reports of the miracles and wonders went beyond being a deliverer. The stories were told how he healed the sick, gave sight to the blind, and even had power over demonic forces.

Last month, she and her husband had traveled down to Gennesaret on business. While he tended to his business, she had walked down to the market-place. There, she heard the reports of the various miracles this man, known as the Master, was doing. She heard how he set free those who were tormented by devils. How her heart leaped to hear that there might be hope for her precious baby girl. She knew she had to try and convince her husband to take her to Jerusalem to meet with the Master.

She had tried everything to help relieve the torment her daughter suffered with. Many nights, she lay awake, while her child lay strapped to a bed, as she thrashed around, oblivious to those around her. As the days wore on, her daughter became more confused, and the violent seizures took hold of her more frequently. The woman sought help from doctors, friends, and even her own religious leaders but none could contribute any relief.

Then the unbelievable happened. News arrived that Jesus had left the Jewish region and had come north to her own area. She began to plan how she would approach him regarding her daughter.

Now as she stood on the sidelines of the crowd, she began to call out to Jesus, "O Lord, son of David, have mercy on my daughter and me!" But he never came out. She cried and pleaded but to no avail. Maybe he couldn't hear her. Maybe he was ignoring her. After all, she was a Canaanite, and Jews were forbidden to associate with the Canaanites, but she refused to give up. After what seemed like hours waiting and calling out to Jesus, she was no closer to him than she had been earlier. The crowd did not budge, and the men continued to stand against the door. She was determined not to give up hope. She decided to go around the side of the house, and maybe she could look inside through a window. As she turned to the corner of the house, a miracle awaited her. She found another door that no one else was near, so she carefully and quietly entered the house.

Chapter 9

As she stepped into the dark quiet house, she heard voices around the corner. It sounded like maybe three or four men talking, and one of them sounded like Jesus. His voice was smooth and soothing yet strong and wise; the others must have been his disciples. She listened as he spoke. "My orders from my Father are to reach the lost children of Israel first. Someday it will be your mission to go to the Gentiles and preach the good news, but until then, I will only do what my Father says to do."

As he was speaking, she quietly turned the corner to look into the small, dark room where they sat. Jesus was seated while the other three men sat on the floor surrounding his feet. As she observed the scene before her, he suddenly looked up and caught her eyes. She noticed that his eyes were dark but gentle. He didn't say anything, and surprisingly, he didn't even look startled to see her standing there. This was her perfect opportunity to ask for help; but suddenly, a peace descended upon her, filling her with hope and faith. She knew he was the Son of God and that nothing was impossible for him. She had never felt such an awesome presence. She ran and knelt at his feet. She began to sob uncontrollably as she worshiped him. The disciples instantly rose to their feet and tried unsuccessfully to remove her, but she kept calling out, "Lord, help me."

He motioned for them to stop and answered her, "It is not good to take the children's bread and throw it to the little dogs."

She responded, "Yes, Lord, yet even the little dogs eat the crumbs which fall from their masters' table."

At that moment, he smiled such a wonderful smile and reached down to help her up. He looked around at the disciples with wonder and amazement in his eyes and then looked down at her and exclaimed, "Oh, woman, great is your faith! Let it be to you as you desire."

She knew at that moment that her daughter was healed. She hugged him tightly as he laughed with her. She thanked him and told him that she would forever be grateful. He smiled and told her to go and sin no more so that a more severe sickness would not come upon her child. She left the little house where the Master was staying with a new-found love and joy. She ran all the way home, her feet barely touching the ground, anticipating what she would find at home and rejoicing at what she had found with Jesus. After all these years of searching for an answer, her search was finally over, not only for the healing of her daughter but for the emptiness and loneliness in her own personal life. She had met the Master, and somehow, she knew that things would be different for her and her family from then on.

Chapter 10

All the way home, she cried and thanked God for what he had done for them. He had done more than just heal her daughter; he had rescued her from a life of pain and sorrow. As she ran home, her mind wandered, and she began to recall the day that the nightmare began in their small humble home.

For centuries, her ancestors had worshipped strange gods. It was common practice to sacrifice children and to perform immoral deeds all in the name of "religion and worship." That was the reason for the hostility between the Israelites and the Canaanites. When her daughter was yet an infant, the elders of her religious sect approached her and her husband explaining that it was necessary to perform a ceremonial dedication to the gods. They were requesting to use their daughter in the traditional ceremony because of her extreme beauty. They explained that this prestigious event would place them in high honor before the people and their gods. They explained to the young couple that no harm would come to the child. She would be placed on an altar in a symbolic manner to worship the god of Molech. Unfortunately, the young couple agreed.

The date was set, and the people of the region began to plan for the traditional, religious festivities. For the event, beautiful dresses were made, decorations were created, and food was prepared. The young couple beamed with pride as people came to observe and admire the beautiful young child that would be a symbolic sacrifice to their god Molech.

Finally, the day arrived to take the child to a ceremonial location up in the hills surrounded by trees. The priests were dressed in fine silk robes, and the people lined up as the couple carried their beautiful child down the center aisle to the altar. Fire burned beneath the altar, but the couple had been assured that their child would be safely placed in a container, high above the fire. As the young father placed the baby into the container, she looked up at him with such love in her big brown eyes, smiling her endearing sweet smile. He leaned over and kissed her forehead and rubbed her cheek. He then turned and stepped down from the altar. It would be several years before he again saw that precious smile and love in those gentle eyes.

The ceremony began, and the rituals were long and tedious with the sound of drums beating wildly. Only the men of the region were allowed close to the outside altar to observe the proceedings. There was a large statue looming behind the altar with the body of a man and the face of an ox. The priest lined up in a circular fashion around the altar. A goblet of goat's blood was passed from one priest to another as they drank from the cup. Long prayers were said, and young woman with flowing scarves danced around the altar with lewd and seductive moves.

Finally, the ceremony was concluded, and the feasting began with the whole congregation participating. The tables were piled with delicious foods and wine. While the musicians played their instruments, the people danced and sang. The child was passed from one priest to another as they each recited a ritual prayer over her.

After a long day, the couple and their child began the journey home. The child lay quietly in her mother's arms as they walked. Her eyes were closed; her breathing was soft as she slept after such an eventful day. The young mother looked down on her sleeping child, admiring her soft and smooth skin as her dark lashes framed her chubby cheeks. When suddenly, the child began to arch her back and let out such a terrifying, piercing scream, the young couple became frightened. They rushed to their home and tried to comfort her, but again, she screamed. She opened her eyes for a few seconds, and there was a look of terror and pain. Gone was the look of love and wonder. The young couple tried unsuccessfully to calm their child down, but nothing helped. She was being severely tormented, and they had no answers. This was only been the beginning of a horrible nightmare that would last for years. Years of searching for help only to be disappointed over and over again. Their beautiful child had been lost to them until now.

All these memories flooded back as she hurried to get to her child and husband. Jesus had said that what she desired would be done for her. She could hardly wait to get home to see the result. When she arrived home, she ran to the door and flung it wide open. For as long as she lived, she would forever recall that precious scene before her. Her husband sat on the floor holding their beloved daughter while she looked up at him with clear, big brown eyes. Her beautiful brown curls bouncing as she giggled and played with him. Suddenly, they both turned and looked at her. Her daughter squealed with delight and exclaimed, "Mommy, you're back, and I feel good." She ran and knelt beside her daughter hugging and laughing with her.

"I know, baby. Jesus made you well. Everything is going to be okay now." The three of them sat there with tears streaming down their faces. Jesus had not only healed her child but had restored life back to them.

Chapter 11

One year had passed since that wonderful day that Jesus changed their life. A year of reconnecting and restoring what had been stolen from them as a family. Each moment treasured and appreciated as they spent it together. The woman was now pregnant with their second child, and she and her husband agreed that this child would be dedicated to the Lord. They no longer attended the temple where their ancestors worshipped. Their prayer time was spent in their home, on their knees, praising God and giving thanks for all he had done for them. They had planned a trip to seek out Jesus and to personally thank him for the healing of their child, but then news had reached them that he had been crucified by his own people. The severity of the news grieved their hearts, and they cried in anguish for the unjust deed.

Strangely enough though, a few days later, a young man approached them whom they had never met. He began explaining to them all that had occurred in Jerusalem since the crucifixion of Jesus. He told them that Jesus had risen from the dead and that there were many confirmed sightings. The religious leaders of the synagogue were in an uproar and were trying to keep the news from escaping, but it was traveling fast. He explained to them the prophecies concerning the Messiah. They were both in awe of his words, and time fled by as he spoke of Jesus Christ the Son of God. He informed them that Jesus had told his disciples to go to Galilee where he would meet with them. Immediately, the young couple gathered their child and a few belongings and began the departure to Galilee.

The journey from Sidon to Galilee was a few days but the time sped by as they discussed all they had heard and received. Soon they would be close to Jesus to thank him for changing their lives.

The morning they arrived in Galilee, there was a small crowd gathered at the sea. The cool morning air was crisp and clear. There was a feeling of anticipation in the atmosphere. There were small groups huddled together, singing and praising God. Suddenly there was a charge in the air and there he stood. His robe was gleaming white, and his voice came across loud and clear.

"He who believes in me the works that I do he will do also and greater works than these he will do because I go to my Father. If you ask anything in my name, I will do it. The Father will give you another Helper that He may abide with you forever. I will not leave you orphans. I will come back to you. It is now time for you to go into the all the world and preach the gospel to every creature. He who believes and is baptized will be saved; but he who does not believe will be condemned. And these signs will follow those who believe. In my name they will cast out demons; they will speak with new tongues; they will take up serpents; and if they drink anything deadly, it will by no means hurt them; they will lay hands on the sick, and they will recover." *He told them that it was important for them all to return to Jerusalem to wait for the Comforter.*

As the young couple and their daughter heard these words, they began to weep. They immediately knelt on the ground and began to worship Jesus. The glorious peace and joy that surrounded them was unlike anything they had ever experienced. For a moment in time, their spirits were quickened with energy. The woman looked up at that moment and saw that Jesus was looking right at her. There was recognition in his eyes as he smiled down at her. She looked back at him with tears streaming down her face and love and gratitude reflected in her eyes. *"Thank you,"* she whispered. She knew that she, too, was now a child of God.

Part 4

I Thirst

Chapter 12

The sun bore down on him on that warm dark day as blood and sweat ran down his face. His eyes were swollen, and his face was bruised. His hair was sticky with dry blood. He was disfigured, and his body was torn, as she looked up to see her beloved Lord, hanging on the cross. He looked down at her, with recognition and love in his eyes. She was at the foot of the cross, heartbroken and weeping when suddenly, he cried out, *"I thirst."* She recalled those same familiar words that he had spoken to her not too long ago, as he sat beside the well where she went to draw water. She recalled that warm evening, in Samaria as though it were just yesterday.

Three years prior

The sun was setting behind the trees as she wearily traveled the narrow and dusty path to Jacob's well. The laughter of small children playing in the nearby streets brought a small, but sad smile to her lips, reminding her of a happier time when her own children were young. As she walked the long steep road to the well, her shoulders stooped under the weight of the heavy water-pot carried on her shoulders.

She had been a beautiful woman, at one time, with long black wavy hair and eyes that sparkled with happiness. Her dark hair was now streaked with gray, and her eyes reflected lifelessness. Her face, once smooth and flawless, was now lined and hard caused by a life filled with pain and rejection.

She usually enjoyed the walk to the well during this time of day. Most of the women from the region had already been to draw water. She avoided the crowd to spare herself from the stares and whispers of the other women. She was judged cruelly for the bad choices and painful life she had led. When she was younger, she had been considered beautiful, and men longed for her company; yet there had always been an emptiness deep down in the pit of her soul. How ironic that every day she walked to draw water and yet she was never able to satisfy the thirst she felt deep down inside, a craving for love and acceptance. For many years, she held onto a dream that someday, she would find a man who would love her for who she was and give her stability and security. She could not recall when she finally came to terms that the man she had been searching for did not exist. The only way she knew to protect herself from getting hurt again was to harden her heart to any man that tried to get close to her. She shook her head to try and shake the thoughts away. No reason to get depressed and saddened by unfulfilled dreams. Such nonsense, to think she actually had thought that someone would care enough to love her. The man she was currently living with, was a decent man. Even though they never spoke of love or commitment, at least she had a roof over her head and food on her table. Still, there was an emptiness to her life.

As she approached the well, she realized that there was a stranger seated close to the well. She hesitated for a moment. Who was the stranger at the well? She had never seen him before in the area. He had long shoulder-length brown hair and seemed to be staring in the distance as though he waited for someone. It reminded her of a deer, straining to hear the sounds of a nearby human. Suddenly, he turned towards her and smiled, the most beautiful smile she had ever seen. It almost seemed, as though, he had been waiting for her. How foolish! He didn't even know her. She looked up into his eyes and experienced a piercing in her soul. She had received stares from many men in her lifetime. Some stared at her with pleasure while others with disgust, but this man looked at her with acceptance. This was strange to her, and it confused her for a moment.

She approached cautiously, avoiding eye contact with the stranger. She lowered her water-pot and began to draw water from the well. She felt, rather than saw, him, watching her every move. Suddenly, he spoke to her, a deep, resounding voice yet kind and gentle. "Please give me a drink, I thirst."

His presence and the sound of his voice discomforted her. He was a Jewish man! What was he doing in this area, talking to her? Why was he being so pleasant to her? What did he want? She immediately put up her emotional guard, turned, and answered him, "Why are you asking me to give you a drink when you are Jewish and I'm a Samaritan woman? Normally, you people don't want to have anything to do with us."

He immediately answered her but not with the response she was expecting. "If you knew the gift of God and who it is who says to you, 'Give me a drink,' you would have asked him, and he would have given you living water."

Now she was perplexed. What was he talking about? "Living water?" She looked at him for a moment before she responded, "Sir, you have nothing to draw with, and the well is deep. Where then do you get that living water? Are you greater than our father Jacob, who gave us the well, and drank from it himself, as well as his sons and his livestock?"

He smiled at her then and began to explain. "Whoever drinks of this water will thirst again, but whoever drinks of the water that I shall give him will never thirst. But the water that I shall give him will become in him a fountain of water springing up into everlasting life."

Suddenly, she began to understand. Could he have somehow read her thoughts? How did he know that she was thirsting for more than what this life had offered her? Could this be the man that had been traveling throughout Israel, healing the sick, and feeding the hungry? Maybe he would perform a miracle for her and give her enough water to last her a lifetime. She would never have to walk the distance to the well and hear the snide remarks from the other women. So she answered him, "Sir, give me this water, that I may not thirst, nor come here to draw."

He said to her, "Go, call your husband and come here."

Oh, wonderful, there was a catch. She would not be able to experience a miracle in her life because she was a sinful woman. She was living with a man but was not married to him. She bowed her head in shame. He must know about her. Here, he was such a good and decent man, knowing that she had led such a shameful and unworthy life. She answered him, "Sir, I have no husband."

She knew that if she lifted her head, she would see the look of disgust in his eyes. Gone would be the kindness and acceptance that had previously been there. He would probably walk away, and her opportunity for a miracle would be gone. But when she looked up, he looked into her eyes and took her hands into his and said, "You have well said, 'I have no husband,' for you have had five husbands, and the one whom you now have is not your husband and never intends to be. In that you spoke truly, I'm glad you were honest."

This was no ordinary man. He understood things about her that no one had ever taken the time to figure out. She hadn't revealed anything about herself, and yet he knew so much. He must be a prophet! She wanted desperately to start doing things right in her life. Maybe, he could help her. So she asked him, "Sir, where is the best place to worship God? Here on this mountain, or do I have to go to Jerusalem?"

He answered her, "It is not here on this mountain or in Jerusalem but true worshipers will worship the Father in spirit and truth; for the Father is seeking such to worship Him. God is Spirit, and those who worship Him must worship in spirit and truth. It isn't where you worship Him but how you worship Him. You must worship Him with all your being."

It suddenly occurred to her that he was more than just a prophet. She said to him, "I know that Messiah is coming. When He comes, He will tell us all things."

He looked deep into her eyes and responded, "I who speak to you am He." He continued looking at her while his words impacted her soul. Then a slow smile came across her face. His eyes lit up as he realized that she understood. He was the long-awaited Messiah! He was the One that everyone had been waiting for. The atmosphere changed, and excitement filled the air. She felt happy as though a heavy burden had been lifted from her shoulders. Tears streamed down her face as she worshiped him. The realization hit her; he had been waiting for her. He knew all about her, and yet he loved her. She had never felt such a deep penetrating love that cleansed her soul and mind. Suddenly nothing else seemed to matter. She sobbed as she knelt before him. She finally felt whole. The longing in her soul vanished, and she wanted nothing but to stay in this perfect place.

Suddenly, there was a commotion behind her. His disciples were returning from the city. She noticed them staring at her, but no one said anything. She stood up shyly, abruptly turning, and ran back down the dusty path, leaving her water-pot behind. She felt light and free as though she were flying. She could barely contain the joy inside of her. She had to tell someone. She ran into the city. Many turned to stare at her as she called out to them. "The Messiah is here and he knows all about me yet he loves me. Come and see for yourselves. He is at the well."

The people were astonished to see the woman who barely said a word to anyone, running and crying out that the Messiah was in their small village. Yet, there was something that caused them to wonder if she might be right. Many had seen her at the well talking to a stranger. The merchants of the village remembered that there had been strangers in the market-place earlier looking to purchase bread and wine. Could this be the Christ? Some left their places of business to seek out the stranger. Others stood indecisive wondering if this, in fact, could be the Messiah. Many marveled at seeing the woman, who, for many years, had an angry and bitter countenance now with joy and hope filling her eyes; it was a miracle in itself.

When many of the villagers arrived at the well, they found Jesus seated, talking to his disciples. They stood around to listen to the words of life that proceeded out of his mouth. He indicated for them to stay and listen. As night began to fall, the woman whom he had spoken to earlier approached and invited Jesus and his disciples to stay at her home. Jesus accepted, and they walked back to her house, followed by a large crowd of villagers.

Chapter 13

For the woman, her life dramatically changed that day. She had the privilege of having Jesus and his disciples stay in her home for two days. Two days filled with joy, peace, and wonder. She listened to every word he spoke, longing for more yet felt full of satisfaction. She hummed songs while she worked preparing meals for the villagers that crowded her home to hear the Master speak. She was busy tending to Jesus and his disciples, yet at night as she lay down to sleep, she was filled with excitement and anticipation to live her life for her Savior. Miraculously, she would awaken refreshed and ready to sit and listen to Jesus as he taught a new way to live.

One night after the others had gone to sleep. Jesus sat outside on the roof looking up towards heaven. She walked quietly up towards him. He turned and motioned for her to sit beside him. It was peaceful to sit beside him in the moonlight. It had been years since she had sensed such comfort and acceptance. They sat quietly together until finally she turned to him and asked him, "Please explain to me what you meant when you said that I would never thirst again."

He smiled at her and responded, "The world offers artificial love with many demands but the only one who offers true love is our Heavenly Father. That is the reason why you searched for so long and could never satisfy the craving inside of you. Now that you know the Father's love, you will never thirst again. Someday I will leave this world, but the Father will send a comforter to fill you so that rivers of living water will flow out of your heart."

She smiled, understanding settling in her eyes. She nodded indicating that she understood but then turned to him and asked him, "Do you ever thirst for anything?"

He responded, "I thirst to do my Father's will, to please Him, and obey Him."

Two days later, as Jesus and his disciples packed up to leave, she stood at the doorway watching them. Jesus came to her and grabbed both her hands in his. He looked into her eyes and said to her. "I am leaving now, but I will be back for you someday. My Spirit will be with you always. Remember, that I love you and my Father in heaven loves you. You are a new creature in Christ. Sin no more."

She answered him, "Jesus, thank you for everything, I will live a life in accordance to your Word, anxiously awaiting your arrival."

He smiled at her as he turned to walk away.

Chapter 14

Since that day, whenever Jesus was in the near vicinity, she would travel to hear his wonderful teachings. She gleaned from his words and memorized what he taught. She had made friends with some of the woman from the village, and together, they would make the journey to hear the teachings from the Master. Often, he would see her in the crowd. He would lift his hand in a wave and smile at her.

One bright spring morning, as she was sweeping her front porch, a young boy came running towards her. As she squinted towards the morning sun, she recognized him as her dear friend Rachel's boy. She stopped sweeping as he approached her. He was out of breath from running and began to convey the message from Rachel, "My mother asked me to come and let you know that they have arrested the Master in Jerusalem. He is being charged with lies and accusations. She and my father are leaving to go to Jerusalem immediately."

She dropped her broom and ran, following the young boy back to his home. There she found Rachel, packing to make the journey to Jerusalem. She called out, "Rachel, you must wait for me, I want to come with you."

Rachel responded, "It is very dangerous to go to Jerusalem right now. I am going and staying with family from my husband's side."

"Please let me come with you," she pleaded.

Rachel saw the look of agony in her friend's face; she knew how much she loved Jesus, so she responded, "Very well, but you must hurry, we don't have much time."

So they immediately left on the journey to Jerusalem. They were silent along the way, deep in thought as to what they would find in Jerusalem.

When they arrived, they saw the crowd and heard the screams and cries at the top of the hill. The scene they found at the top of the hill was horrifying. There, the Master hung on a cross between two thieves. His body was badly beaten and bloody. Mary, his mother, weeping, hovered near the cross, with John and the other Mary standing close by. The Roman soldiers stood around in a circle, mocking and laughing. What had they done to her Lord? What was happening? Rachel held her close and tried to comfort her. "We must not make a commotion. We don't know what the soldiers will do next. Come, let us get closer to the cross."

As they approached the cross, Jesus turned his head towards her. She looked up into the eyes of her Savior. He was unrecognizable, except for His eyes. They still looked into her soul with love and compassion. Why was this happening to him? Who would do such a cruel and evil thing to her Lord? Suddenly, Jesus' words came back to her. "I am the Good Shepherd and I lay down my life for my sheep. No one takes it from me, but I lay it down of myself." She also remembered him, saying, "I am the resurrection and the life. He who believes in me, though he may die, he shall live."

Suddenly it was as though everything made sense to her. She understood what he had been saying all this time. He was giving his life to cancel her debt, but he would rise again because he was life. She looked up to see him watching her, and he nodded his head, confirming what she was thinking.

As she stayed that day at the cross watching her Master give his life for the world, she thought of many things. She remembered his smile and laughter, his courage and compassion. She recalled how the crowd would reach out to touch him, and he would graciously touch their hands and hold their children. He often would stop what he was saying to touch a crying child and heal a dying grandmother. He offered love and hope to the weak and distraught.

Now here he was, dying like a common criminal with no dignity or recognition. She vowed on that day to keep his message alive. She bowed down at the foot of the cross. The soldiers watched her as she wept, touching the blood-stained cross. Blood dripped off his feet and fell on her garment as her shoulders shook with deep sobs from her innermost being. The agony of watching her Savior die was overwhelming but necessary. She wanted to remember this day forever. To have it ingrained in her spirit so that she would always appreciate his sacrifice for her. She understood that history was being played out right before her eyes and life, as she knew it, would never be the same. He had promised her that he would come back for her someday, and she held to that promise as she heard his final words. "It is finished." He had been born to die for an unworthy world. His thirst to do the will of the Father was accomplished.

Part 5

At His Feet

Chapter 15

Mary quickened her pace as she pressed through the crowd of shoppers at the market-place. She had been up since dawn preparing for this evening's event; she had been anticipating this day for weeks ever since she heard that the Master was coming to their home.

Mary lived in Bethany, a small village approximately five miles from Jerusalem. She lived with her sister Martha and her brother Lazarus. Jesus would often stop by their home to sit and visit with them. The moment news went out that Jesus was in town, everyone from the nearby vicinity would congregate at their home, to hear the precious teachings that Jesus would speak. Mary would take her place at the feet of Jesus, to sit and listen to the words that he spoke. His teachings would reach down into her innermost being and bring life to her parched soul.

She recalled the first time she had gone into the room, where the men gathered to listen to Jesus speak. There were those who spoke against the fact that she would come into the room where the men were seated. Jesus looking into her eyes with that look that penetrated her soul rebuked those that murmured against her. He then invited her to be seated at his feet; from that day forward, that is where she sat with him.

As she arrived home with her purchases, she found Martha with a worried look on her face.

"Mary," Martha exclaimed, "what took you so long? The Master will be here any minute. Please, help me finish preparing this meal!" Martha was the worrier of the two sisters, but Mary loved her with all her heart.

Mary reached over and put her arms around Martha, laughing as she said, "Oh, Martha, everything will turn out fine. Jesus always loves your cooking. Besides you know how he's always saying, 'Be anxious for nothing.' Now let me help you until he arrives."

Martha gave her sister a loving smile and knew she was right. She couldn't stop her sister from sitting with the Lord. She certainly did not want Jesus to rebuke her again because of her *"worries."* She went back to her work, anxiously awaiting the arrival of Jesus.

When Mary heard the crowd approaching, she ran to the open door to await the arrival of Jesus. He saw her waiting for him and smiled as he raised his hand to wave to her. His disciples tried to keep the crowd from pressing upon him, but Jesus would reach out and touch their hands as they held them out to him. He was always very loving and kind. It did not matter if they were rich or poor, young or old, male or female; he loved them all. When Jesus arrived at the door, Lazarus rushed out to greet him with a big embrace and an invitation to come inside. Martha and Mary also came over to greet the Lord with smiles and embraces. The disciples followed Jesus into the loving home of Lazarus and his sisters.

It was a pleasant home with sunlight beaming through the windows. The house had been scrubbed clean, and the delicious aroma of lamb stew penetrated throughout the house. Jesus looked around the house and smiled; he knew that he was loved and welcomed in this home.

Jesus' disciples were a boisterous bunch, but they were dedicated to the Lord. Mary watched how they made sure he was comfortable and if he needed anything. Jesus always had a kind word and smile to give to them. After everyone had greeted each other and were seated around the room, Jesus began to speak. Immediately, the room became quiet, and a glorious peace filled the room. There was anticipation and wonder on the faces who listened to the Master. Mary ran to take her place at his feet as he continued in his gentle and kind way. For a few hours, life would stand still for those in the house in the little town of Bethany.

Chapter 16

For three years, Mary and her family had followed and supported the ministry of Jesus. It had been a wonderful time. Jesus would often lodge in their home and bring hope and joy into their lives; but suddenly, tragedy had struck.

Mary sat stunned in silence in her home; she could not believe that Lazarus was dead. Lazarus had been like a father to her after her own had passed away. He loved and protected her and Martha. He was strong and wise, always looking to provide the best for them— and now he was gone. Their lives had been turned upside down.

A few days earlier, Lazarus had complained of a headache. Martha quickly directed him to lie down. He was feverish, and Martha laid cool, wet towels on his forehead. As the night wore on, Lazarus seemed to be getting worse. In the morning, Martha asked Mary to summon a messenger to let Jesus know that Lazarus was ill. Surely, Jesus would hasten to come to his friend who was in need; but Jesus never came, and Lazarus had died a few days later.

Something was not right. What was going on? These questions and others passed through Mary's mind that dark spring day. She had seen Jesus perform countless of miracles, and yet now that they had needed one, it seemed as though he had forgotten them. He had promised never to leave them nor forsake them, but where was he? Mary shook her head as though to clear her mind. She could not give up now. She had heard, seen, and received enough from Jesus to know that he was faithful. She decided to refuse to give in to the fear and trust the Lord. Suddenly, she knew that he would come through.

Mary waited, recalling the words she heard Jesus speak. "Nothing is impossible with God." Those words kept replaying in her mind until they were saturated in her spirit. Mary did not want to talk to anyone. She sat silently waiting. She knew that Martha and her family and friends were worried about her, but it was the only way she knew to keep the fear and sorrow from gripping her heart. She remembered Jesus saying to Jairus, the official, when his daughter had died. "Fear not, only believe." He then had gone into the house and had resurrected Jairus's daughter back to life. What a wonderful miracle. The word had spread that Jesus had the power to restore life to the dead. Would he do that for Lazarus? Jesus had changed lives and had brought comfort and hope to many. Mary had sat at his feet hearing and receiving his words of love. So now she waited.

It had been four days, and still, Mary waited. Jesus would come. When or how, she was not sure. But when he did, everything was going to be alright. Suddenly, Mary heard a commotion outside.

Martha ran in and grabbed her by the arms. "Mary," she exclaimed, "the Master is her and he is asking for you."

Without hesitating, Mary ran out to meet Jesus. He was still a mile from her house, but she did not care. She ran to him, dust gathering at her feet as she hurried through the streets of Bethany to her Lord, and there he was, waiting for her. As it was her custom, she fell at his feet.

Immediately, she began to sob with tears streaming down her face. She cried out, "Master, had you been here, my brother would not have died."

Jesus groaned deep within himself and leaned down to gently stroke her hair as he asked, "Where have you laid him?"

As Mary rose to her feet, Martha and a few close friends arrived, responding to Jesus' question. They began to walk towards the place where Lazarus was buried.

The burial site was on a steep, mountainous terrain. The small crowd climbed the hilly mountain side with caution. No one spoke a word, the only sound heard was of loose pebbles, crunching under the feet of the small group. A large, black crow flew above them screaming a loud shrill as he flew away. The white stones surrounding the tomb glared in the hot sun causing the onlookers to squint and shade their eyes with their hands. The eeriness of death hovered over the atmosphere where the dead lay. When Jesus arrived at the tomb, he looked around, examining what lay before him. There was a challenge in the air as though life and death stood face to face. Suddenly, Jesus turned towards the giant stone that covered the cave and said, *"Remove the stone."*

There was a loud gasp and then silence. Finally, Martha spoke up, "Lord, it has been four days since we buried my brother. Surely by now, his body is decaying and it stinks."

But Jesus turned to Martha and said, "Did I not tell you that if you believe, you shall see the glory of God?"

Martha lowered her eyes from Jesus' intense look and said, "Yes, Lord, I believe." She then motioned for the men to remove the stone.

Mary watched all of this in silence. Suddenly, a great peace came over her. The atmosphere changed as a charge filled the air. She knew she was about to witness a great miracle. She turned to see Jesus raise his eyes toward heaven and say, "Father, I know that you always hear me but so that these that are here will believe that you sent me, I come to you now."

He then called out with a loud voice, "Lazarus, come forth."

Time stood still for a moment. Everyone stared at the open tomb. No one said a word. No one moved a muscle, when suddenly from the cave, bound up in the traditional wrappings for the dead, came Lazarus. For an instant, Mary could not move. She stood in awe as she witnessed the unbelievable; Jesus had power over death. Nothing was impossible for him. She heard as the Lord told them to loose the bandages that bound her brother.

Martha rushed with the others to do as Jesus commanded. She then wrapped her arms around Lazarus as she cried and laughed with him. But Mary bowed her head and with tears of love and gratitude coming down her face. Her knees were weak as she walked toward the Lord. He was watching the group gathered around Lazarus as they joyfully untied him, but as she got closer to him, he turned and smiled at her. She fell at his feet with love and devotion and cried at the feet of Jesus, thanking him for returning to them their brother.

Chapter 17

One week had passed since that glorious day that Jesus had raised Lazarus from the dead. It had been a week of celebration and awe. Visitors from all over the area had heard of the miraculous deed and were curious to see the man that had been dead and was now alive. For Mary, the events of the past week had confirmed what she had known all along. Jesus was not only a good man living uprightly and working righteousness. He was truly the Son of God, the long-awaited Messiah. Mary was so grateful to Jesus for what he had done for them that she wanted to give him something in appreciation. She thought long and hard and finally decided on a gift. When Mary's parents had passed away, they had left a small inheritance to their children. Lazarus had advised Mary and Martha to invest their inheritance in oil and an alabaster box (a costly marble container for oil) and to save it for use as a dowry, so that is exactly what they had done. Now Mary brought out that precious ointment that was kept inside the beautiful box.

She remembered vividly the day she and Martha had purchased the alabaster box with its rich ointment. They had risen early in the morning and had traveled to Jerusalem to the great market-place in the city. There, merchants from different parts of the world would bring their goods to barter or trade with the residents of the area. After hours of searching, Mary's eyes finally fell on the box she had been looking for. It was wonderful, like nothing she had ever seen. It was a heavy box made of alabaster. Mary could see that the maker had spent precious time carving the intricate detail into the outside of the box. Inside of the box was a small vial that contained expensive oil that had the most wonderful scent she had ever smelled. She felt like a queen as she held this box in her hands. She took it home and wrapped it in a silk cloth to wait for the day that someone would choose her to be his bride.

Today Mary pulled out the beautiful alabaster box. She knew what she had to do. Suddenly, everything seemed so clear. It is though she finally understood what Jesus had been saying all along. It all came to her the day that he raised her brother from the dead. She remembered the words that he spoke that day, "I am the resurrection and the life."

Mary realized that in order for someone to be resurrected, they had to die first. She now understood that Jesus was the sacrificial lamb for all mankind. He was sent from the Father above to die so that all could live. In a few days, the Passover celebrations would begin. She knew that Jesus' time was near. Today she would let Jesus know that she understood what he was about to do. She felt excitement and wonder that the mystery of the Scriptures was about to be unveiled and, for some unknown reason, to her, she was a small participant to this wonderful event.

She smiled as she held the precious box to her heart. She gently laid the box down and wrapped it back up in the silk cloth. She turned and began to brush her long golden brown hair; she brushed it until it shone. She was thinking of all the wonderful things she had experienced since Jesus had come into their lives. She had seen great miracles and had heard wonderful teachings, and yet he was about to do the greatest wonder of all. She had to hurry; Jesus and his disciples would be gathering at the house where a celebration was to be held for the resurrection of Lazarus. She wrapped her hair at the nape of her neck, grabbed her shawl, and picked up the silk cloth with its precious cargo.

Chapter 18

The celebration was being held in Bethany, in honor of the resurrection of Lazarus. Jesus had been invited, along with other friends and family. Martha had been up since dawn preparing a wonderful meal. It was a day of rejoicing and thankfulness for the wonderful blessing that Jesus had given to them.

As Mary approached the house where the meal was to take place, she saw that it was already crowded with well wishers and onlookers. Mary noticed a group of religious leaders lingering along the side of the house, watching and whispering among them. They watched her as she passed them; bowing her head, she hurried up the steps to the house. There were rumors among the people that some of the religious leaders were seeking a way to arrest Jesus and to put an end to the miracles. They were concerned because of his large circle of influence and feared a revolt. Mary finally approached the door to the house and opened it.

It took a moment for her eyes to adjust from the bright sunlight outside to the dimly lit room inside. The room was crowded with people. Jesus sat over in a corner with a group of men surrounding him as they took in his teachings and his words. Mary stood at the entry way, taking in the scene. Suddenly, Jesus turned to her, looking right into her eyes and motioned for her to come near. It occurred to Mary at that moment that he also knew why she was here.

As she moved toward Jesus, she was well aware of the occupants of the room staring at her. She held her precious alabaster box close to her and began to unwrap the silk cloth from around the box. When she arrived to the place where Jesus was seated, she knelt before him and began to remove his sandals from his feet. His feet were dusty from his journey and callused from his long walks along the byways. She then loosed her hair from its knot at her neck and began to dust off his feet. She then broke open the seal to the alabaster box and began to rub and massage his precious feet with the sweet smelling oil. She looked up once to see Jesus and noticed him smiling down at her. She stood up then and went behind him to pour the oil upon his head. She remembered the Psalm that stated, "It is like the precious oil upon the head, running down on the beard, the beard of Aaron." He leaned his head back and allowed the oil to run down his hair. Everyone watched with curiosity and wonder. But there were those who were angered by the demonstration. The precious aroma filled the room, and Mary continued pouring the oil. She wept as she poured the oil. She cried with gratitude but also because she knew that she had been given the privilege to anoint his body for burial. She understood that too many, this act made no sense, but she was comforted in the fact that Jesus understood her reason. As she poured the last drops of oil on his head, she knelt again at his feet and wiped them with her hair. It was a gesture of love and gratitude but also one of faith.

Suddenly, someone came up from behind her and grabbed her arm to pull her away. Jesus immediately stopped him. It was Judas, one of the disciples. He began to question her and ask why this ointment was not sold and the money given to the poor. Jesus turned to him and said, "Leave her alone, she has done this for the day of my burial. The poor you will always have but me you won't always have."

Jesus then turned to Mary and held her hands in his and said, "Mary, everyone will always remember what you have done today, especially me, Thank you."

That was the last time Jesus spoke to Mary before he went to the cross.

Chapter 19

It had been a turbulent week. It all started immediately following the celebration dinner. A local boy had come to tell Lazarus that the religious leaders were seeking to put an end to the story of his resurrection. Jesus told Lazarus to gather his sisters and to head for Galilee. He instructed them to stay there and to wait for him. They immediately gathered a few belongings and left to Galilee that same evening. Later that week, there were reports that Jesus had been arrested and then the unthinkable that he had been crucified. Mary heard all of this, and yet she knew that it was not over. Jesus always had victory, even over death. It was just a matter of time. If Jesus told them to come to Galilee to wait for him, then he had every intention to meet them there. Jesus always kept his word.

A few days later, excitement began to run through the village. The latest news was that Jesus was no longer in the tomb. Some said that his disciples had stolen his body in the night; while others said that he had raised himself from the dead. There was an uproar in the Roman government and dread with the religious leaders. What had happened to Jesus' body? But Mary knew, he was alive and on his way to Galilee. Mary waited anxiously for his arrival.

Days went by, and then early one morning, Martha came in and woke Mary up and said, "Time to get up. Peter, James, and John are here, and they want Lazarus and us to meet them by the sea."

Mary arose and dressed quickly. Today was the day that she had been anticipating. She hurried as she walked with Martha and Lazarus to the Sea of Galilee.

As they approached the shore, there was already a crowd forming at the edge of the water. The sea seemed a deeper blue as the early morning light shimmered across its waters. The sky had a few pink and white clouds scattered across it. It was a beautiful morning. Someone was cooking fish along the shore, and the aroma filled the morning air. Suddenly, Jesus was standing in the midst of them. Everyone stopped and turned to the Master. He was beautiful. His gown was whiter than white, and his face shone like the sun. He then turned to Mary, Martha, and Lazarus and smiled his familiar smile while motioning for them to come closer. Jesus was alive! He was unstoppable. He began to tell the people that he would ascend into heaven and someday, he would return. But until then, they would take this Good News to the ends of the world. He was telling them to return to Jerusalem and wait for the Comforter who would baptize them with the Holy Spirit to empower them to preach the gospel. He said that they would do greater works than he did. For those who believe, they would lay their hands on the sick and they would be healed, they would cast out demons in his name. It was fascinating! Mary listened intently; she knew life would never be the same. She had a mission to do. She owed it to the Lord to obey him. What a wonderful privilege Jesus was giving to her. She bowed down and worshiped him at his feet.

Part 6

Who Touched Me?

Chapter 20

From her window, she could see the morning sun filling the sky. There were small drops of dew on the tree outside of her window. She lay in her bed listening, to the birds chirping and the people bustling about preparing for another day. She recalled how years ago, before the dreaded disease had consumed her life, she too would wake up ready for a new day. Life had been full, full of promise and hope. Now as she lay in her bed, getting up was a task in itself. She lifted herself up and sat at the edge of the bed as a wave of nausea and dizziness swept over her. She waited the episode out and then slowly stood to her feet. As she stood, the blood flowed out of her. It was a curse that tormented her every day.

When her husband had passed away, he had left her with a small fortune; but every bit of it had gone to various types of physicians and specialist to try and bring some relief. No one had a cure. To make matters worse, according to the law, she was considered unclean and therefore could not associate with the general public. She was doomed to a life of seclusion and embarrassment. Not to mention all the torment she felt physically.

She stood standing at the edge of her bed until she felt capable to take a few steps. She no longer slept through the night; even though she was tired, she was unable to rest because of her condition. She slowly walked toward the wash basin where her fifteen-year-old granddaughter Sarah had left fresh water, oil and a towel.

Sarah was her delight; she was the daughter of her eldest son and the most loveable, happy, beautiful little girl she had ever known. After her husband had passed away, her eldest son and his wife had insisted that she come live with them. Sarah was their only daughter. Every night, Sarah would come into her room and talk to her about her day. Lately, she had been telling her grandmother all about a man named Jesus who was going around the region performing great miracles.

How he would touch the sick and they would be healed. She spoke of how the blind, deaf, and dumb were healed. Even the lepers were made whole. Excitedly, Sarah spoke of the wonderful stories she was hearing as her grandmother listened with awe. Many said he was the long awaited Messiah. Sarah insisted that if she could get her grandmother to Jesus, he would heal her. The more she heard of Jesus, the more she believed that he could heal her. If only she could get close enough to at least touch him. But he was a busy man, with multitudes following him, and she was confined to this house. If she attempted to go out looking for him, someone might see her, and she would cause shame to come upon her family. But every day that Sarah shared some news of another healing, her desire to approach this man called Jesus, grew. He must truly be a man of God, to have such power to heal the sick. What she needed was for Jesus to be close enough to touch. What she needed was a miracle. Now as she slowly made her way toward the basin, Sarah burst into her room. "Grandmother, you're up! Guess what? You know how I'm always telling you about Jesus? He is headed toward our village! Yesterday he was in Gadarene, and you know what? The mad man that lives in the cemetery was healed!! He has been seen sitting down and conversing with Jesus. No longer does he look like a deranged animal but a normal human being. Grandmother, if he can heal a mad man, he can surely heal you."

Breathlessly, Sarah stood at the doorway of her grandmother's room. Her eyes were wide with anticipation as she waited for her grandmother's reaction. Her grandmother looked at her with amazement showing on her face. She knew of the man that Sarah spoke of. He had been an intelligent, rational human being who suddenly had become animalistic and depraved. She recalled, at one occasion, on seeing the mad-man from Gadarene. He was chained and foaming at the mouth. He grunted and growled as onlookers walked by. Many said that he was the son of the devil, and he looked it. His hair was matted, and he was filthy.

"Sarah, he's coming to our village? If he healed the madman, he can heal me. I need for you to help to get to Jesus while he is this close."

"Oh, Grandmother, I know he can heal you too. I have a plan. We could cover your face, so no one would know it was you. You could then work your way through the crowd to get close enough to Jesus."

She pondered this plan of Sarah's for a while. If Jesus could heal a mad-man, he certainly had enough power to heal her of her infirmity. All she would need to do is touch him, and no one would need to know that she had been there. It was settled. Now that he was this close, she could not miss her opportunity.

"Okay. Sarah, let's do it. Take me to Jesus."

"Oh, Grandmother, I just know your life will be changed. Hurry, get dressed. We'll leave as soon as you're ready."

Sarah, excitedly closed the door behind her, leaving her grandmother contemplating what she was about to do.

"Oh, God, help me get close enough to touch him." Suddenly, a wonderful peace settled over her. She hurried to get ready, something wonderful was about to happen.

Chapter 21

Thirty minutes later, they were walking the streets of the village. It was a beautiful day with the sun shining brightly. It felt wonderful to be outside again, breathing in the fresh air and feeling the warmth of the sun. Sarah walked beside her grandmother holding her arm. Her eyes sparkled with anticipation believing in her heart that her beloved grandmother would be healed. Her grandmother walked slowly through the streets with her head and face covered. All she could think about was that she needed to get close enough to Jesus to touch him. So many years of bondage had taken its toll. She longed for the ability to enjoy life free from limitations and illness. She thought of how wonderful to walk to the market-place without guilt, to cook and clean her own home without fainting from weakness, or to sit and enjoy conversing with her family without shame. She thought about all the wonderful stories that Sarah had shared with her of others who had been healed. She knew that Jesus was her answer to have her life back.

As the pair silently walked, they began to hear the crowd that followed Jesus. As they turned the corner, they saw the throng of people moving, following a group of men. The two women merged into the crowd, becoming part of the throng. The crowd pressed about them, everyone was trying to get closer to the Master. Her mind raced as she thought of how she was going to get close enough to Jesus to touch him. Suddenly, the crowd stopped. People began whispering that a high official was talking to Jesus. Someone said that it was Jairus, a ruler of the synagogue and that his young daughter was ill. This was her opportunity. She could crawl through the crowd and come up from behind. She would touch the hem of his garment and immediately turn back into the crowd. No one would ever see her. That's when she turned to Sarah and said, "While he is busy speaking to this ruler, I am going to crawl up from behind. I know that all I need to do is touch him, and I will be made whole. Wait here for me, I'll be right back."

Sarah nodded, as she watched her grandmother get down on all fours and began the journey to the front of the crowd, to where Jesus stood, talking to Jairus.

As she crawled through the crowd, she was stepped on and pushed down by the multitude of people, but she would pull herself up and continue crawling. She occasionally had to stop and gasp for air, regaining her composure; she would continue her journey toward her healing. The street was dirty, and her knees and palms became scraped from the rocks that lined the street. But she had come this far, and she was determined to touch Jesus. She had suffered for too long, and this was her last hope, to get close enough to touch him.

She was completely focused on reaching Jesus when suddenly, she looked up and there stood Jesus. He was a tall man, with strong hands. His back was to her as he listened intently while Jairus wept before him. He leaned forward, focusing on what Jairus was saying. The multitude pressed against her, attempting to hold her back from moving forward. In desperation, she reached out and touched the hem of his garment. Immediately she felt a shock run from her fingers, up her arm, and down her body. It was a tingling sensation that flowed throughout her being. She realized at that moment that the flow of blood had stopped! It was amazing. There was no doubt, she was healed. She wanted to shout and dance; but instead, she discretely turned around to crawl back into the crowd when she heard him ask, "Who touched me?"

Those simple words caused her to stop in her tracks. Immediately, his disciples began to explain to him that the crowd was pushing and it was difficult to keep them from touching him. But he was adamant that someone had touched him. She heard him exclaim, "I felt power flow out of me." He turned. And immediately, his eyes looked straight into the eyes of the woman. He asked again while staring into her soul, "Who touched me?"

At that moment, she stepped out of the crowd, trembling and fell down before him, saying, "Oh, Master, it was me, I touched you. I tried to approach you without anyone noticing because I was so ashamed of my illness. But I knew that if I could touch you, I would be made well. The moment my hand reached out to you, I felt your power flow through me, and I was made whole."

He then reached down to help her up. He smiled the warmest smile she had ever seen, "My daughter, live happily. Your faith has made you well. Don't crawl back into the crowd, but go in peace and enjoy your life." He then turned back to Jairus and followed him to his home.

She turned and ran back to Sarah. The crowd stared at her as she ran past them, smiling and reaching out their hands to touch her. If only they too could experience the power of God. But she headed straight for Sarah. Her feet hardly touched the ground as she ran. She felt free and alive. Gone was the nausea and dizziness. No longer did her abdomen feel tender. The discomfort she had experienced was gone. She was a whole woman again, free from the curse of her infirmity.

As she approached Sarah, tears were streaming down both their faces. They hugged each other and began talking and laughing at the same time. Sarah jumped up and down exclaiming, "I knew you would be healed. Oh, Grandmother, tell me everything he said to you."

Her grandmother held on tightly, praising God and thanking him for every good gift, "Thank you, God, for my healing and for the faith of my granddaughter."

She was a blessed woman, and life was good.

Chapter 22

Two years had passed since that wonderful day that she encountered the Lord. For her, the touch that changed her life had not only been a physical touch but more so a spiritual touch. Since that day, she had enjoyed life to its fullest. She hardly stayed home anymore, anxious and excited to be out of the confines of her room.

Sarah and her grandmother frequently followed the Master to nearby regions to hear the life-changing teachings and experience the peace of being close to Jesus. She had never experienced anything like it. There was excitement in the air, generated by the signs and wonders that were evident everywhere Jesus went. It amazed her that he could remember them out of so many people, but then again, he remembered everyone. He was so gracious and loving. He always made one feel as though they were his close friends. Of course, he continued to perform the wonderful healings and miracles throughout their region, and the multitudes followed him everywhere.

Often, he would stop to say hello and ask how she was doing. He had a special way of holding her hands and looking into her heart as he spoke to her. Sarah would often make him laugh with her energy and excitement. Once, the woman asked him how was it that he knew that she was the one who had touched him. He had responded with a gentle smile. "I know when someone is groping for me because I can feel the power of God flowing out of me." Then he said something strange. "It is important that you continue to touch me. I will always know when you do."

"But how do I do that, Lord?" she asked.

He responded, "When you believe for the impossible. That touches me and power will flow from me."

The woman smiled recalling these experiences. She was a different woman with a new-found love and faith. Life was exciting and enjoyable. She owed everything to Jesus. She busied herself preparing

93

for the upcoming Passover celebration and thought how just a couple of years ago, she never would have been able to do the things she was doing now. She never thought that life could be so good in her golden years. As she mixed the flour for the bread she was baking, she thought of how Sarah was growing up to be a lovely woman full of God's grace and wisdom. Her son and his wife became believers soon after seeing the manifestation of her healing and hearing her testimony. Her mind was full of praise to God when Sarah suddenly burst through the door in tears.

"Sarah, what is it? What's wrong?"

Sarah responded, barely able to speak. "Grandmother, they've arrested him! They want to kill him."

Her grandmother looked at her with a horrified expression on her face. What was Sarah talking about? "Sarah, who did they arrest?"

"Jesus, Grandmother. They've arrested Jesus in Jerusalem. Everyone is talking about it down at the market-place. The talk is that they want to crucify him."

Her grandmother slumped down to the floor. Covering her face with her hands, she began to weep. Suddenly, the hour became dark. How could this be? Jesus who went about doing good was being punished for evil things he did not do. She knew that it must have been the religious leaders who had finally arrested her precious Lord. For some time now, there had been talk that they were plotting to arrest him for blasphemy. But the truth be told, the religious leaders were jealous and fearful of Jesus. Sarah knelt down beside her, hugging her close while they both cried and prayed. After the tears were shed, they sat quietly wondering what to do next. Finally, the woman stood up. She wiped the tears from her face and boldly said, "Sarah, I am going down to Jerusalem. I will not sit here crying while my Lord is being tortured. I want him to know that I believe in him. I sense an urgency to be there."

"Okay, Grandmother, but I am coming with you," Sarah responded. "I won't let you go down there alone, at a time like this."

Chapter 22

"We must hurry, Sarah. There isn't much time."

Sarah and her grandmother immediately began making preparations to leave for Jerusalem. Many people from their region were traveling to Jerusalem for the Passover celebration, but Sarah's father insisted on traveling with them so that they would not be alone. Sarah's mother prepared a lunch for their trip, and everything was packed and bundled on their mule. A few hours later, they began their journey to Jerusalem.

Chapter 23

Several hours later, they arrived in Jerusalem. The streets were lined with crowds of people gathering for the Passover celebration. It did not take long for them to hear the news that was being whispered among the people. A crucifixion was taking place outside the city gates on a hill called Golgotha, the place of the *skull*.

As they made their way through the streets of Jerusalem heading toward Golgotha, neither of them said a word. All three were thinking of what was happening up ahead. The crowd was noisy and boisterous moving toward the horrific scene at the top of the hill. There was a charge in the air as evil filled the hearts and minds of the rowdy spectators. Sarah, her father, and grandmother silently climbed the rocky hill. Each noted the blood splattered along the way. When they arrived at the top of the hill, Sarah gasped and cried into her father's outstretched arms while her grandmother looked on at her Master ripped off his dignity. He was between two other men—criminals— no doubt, hanging on a cross.

The woman saw Jesus' mother huddled nearby with two other women and a young man who she recognized as one of his disciples. There were five or six groups of people scattered around silently weeping. The Roman soldiers sat underneath the cross laughing and playing drunken games while religious leaders stood in a group together looking on with arrogance and hate. The rest of the crowd stood off to the side of the crosses, mesmerized by the horrific ordeal. Dark clouds began to form in the sky, and sprinkles of rain fell among the spectators; but still, the woman continued to absorb the scene around her.

She looked up to see Jesus looking at her. His face was swollen and badly beaten, covered with blood and grime. His flesh was torn off his body, and he was covered in blood. Blood was everywhere, flowing freely from his wounds. The wood of the cross was stained with his blood. Puddles of blood were on the ground below the cross.

Never had she seen so much blood...or had she? That's when she realized that because of the blood that was now being shed, she was delivered from her issue of blood. He was doing all of this for her! He had taken her place, shedding his blood. She recalled him saying that he would give his life for his sheep. She did not understand what he was saying at the time, but suddenly, it all made sense. As she looked up into his eyes, he once again looked into her soul, and she heard him call out, "Father, into thy hands I commit my Spirit." She saw him take his last breath and bow his head.

Immediately, lightening flashed, and thunder roared; great drops of rain began to fall. The ground shook as onlookers turned their faces toward the sky with fear in their eyes while others merely ran for cover. But the woman knelt down on the rocky hill and cried, oblivious to the small stones cutting into the flesh of her knees. She cried for what they had done to her Savior, and she cried for what he had done for her. Her sobs came from deep within her soul. She wept until there were no tears left when suddenly, a wonderful peace settled over her. A beautiful presence enveloped her as she knelt on the rocky hill. Slowly, she began to understand that all of this was necessary to fulfill the Scriptures. She needed to have faith in his promise that he would rise again just like she had faith long ago that she could be healed. She never imagined that the first time she touched him was the door for him to come into her life to touch her body, her soul, and her spirit. This was not the end but only the beginning of a wonderful new phase. It was important to continue to believe that nothing was impossible. She recalled the words that he spoke to her that day that she was healed. "Daughter, be of good cheer, your faith has made you well. Go in peace."

With his words resounding in her spirit, she stood up from the ground and wiped the tears from her face. If faith had brought her healing, then faith could see her through this time of despair. She would go in peace and live for her Lord. She pulled Sarah close to her and placed her arm on her son. "Come, my children. We must go in peace. We must believe that he is able to turn this terrible event into something good."

Carrying that truth in their hearts, they began their descent down the rocky hill.

Part 7

Mary

Chapter 24

It was a beautiful sunny afternoon as Mary prepared for the upcoming Passover celebration. The light breeze came through the open window where Mary distractedly worked in her home thinking of the supper she would share with her children later that evening. It was a custom in their family for Mary, her children, and their families to share the Passover supper in Mary's sister's home in Jerusalem. While she busily arranged the ingredients for the unleavened bread she was to bake, her mind wandered to an incident that occurred earlier that morning. Mary's eldest son, Jesus, had come by to inform her that he would not be attending the supper that evening. As she silently assisted her sister in preparing the meal, she recalled his visit. He seemed quiet and pensive as he explained to her that he would be hosting his own Passover supper for his closest friends, his disciples, as he called them. He had made arrangements to have the supper at a friend's home in their upper room. In the past few years, Jesus had become busy in his ministry and did not often participate in family gatherings, but this was odd. Something was different about him today, and she couldn't quite put her finger on it. When she questioned him about it, he merely responded, "My peace I leave with you. Let not your heart be troubled."

As she pondered his visit, memories of her first-born suddenly flooded her mind. The conception and birth of her first-born had been like no other. She often wondered why she was chosen for the awesome task. She would never forget the day thirty-four years ago when she received a visit from heaven. She was still a young girl, not yet married to Joseph, her husband. She often would go up to the rooftop of her parents' home to pray and meditate.

This one particular day, she had been dozing off when suddenly, a tall, powerful man had appeared to her. At first, she thought she might be dreaming, but then a light breeze had brushed her cheek; and she knew she was awake. He said that his name was Gabriel and that he had been sent by the Lord to deliver a message. Mary began to shake with fear, but he stretched out his hand and told her not to be afraid. A great calm fell upon her, and she was able to listen distinctly to what he was saying. He explained that she had found favor in the eyes of God and would give birth to a son. She would call his name Jesus, for he would be the Savior of the world. When she presented the obvious question that was pertinent in her mind that she was still a virgin, he replied that the Holy Spirit would overshadow her to conceive this child. He then told her that her cousin Elizabeth was, even now, six months pregnant. Mary knew that this was a great miracle; Elizabeth had been barren for many years. She then responded, "Be it unto me according to thy word." Humbly, she lowered her head. And when she raised it again, he was gone.

Mary sat on the rooftop for several hours after her visitor was gone. She thought about the news that she had received and of Joseph, her betrothed. How was she ever going to explain this to her family? Would her parents believe her? What about Joseph? He was a good man with great integrity. Would he believe her story of her heavenly visitor and the news that he brought with him? Mary decided to pay Elizabeth a visit. She might have some answers for Mary. Maybe she too had been visited by Gabriel. Mary went downstairs to discuss with her parents her plans to visit Elizabeth.

Chapter 25

The visit from the angel had been the beginning of many extraordinary occurrences that would soon follow. Immediately after speaking with her parents, Mary journeyed to the hill country of Judea to visit with Elizabeth. Elizabeth had also received a visit from heaven. When Mary arrived at Elizabeth's home, she reached over to embrace her cousin. At that moment, the baby in Elizabeth's womb leaped and was filled with the Holy Ghost. It was a wonderful time of rejoicing and gladness. They would sit for hours discussing and analyzing the events that were occurring. Elizabeth helped Mary understand the changes that were happening within her. She was a constant comfort. Mary had many questions, and Elizabeth would assure her that God would work everything out.

After leaving Elizabeth's home, she decided it was time to discuss with her parents and Joseph what was occurring in her own life. Initially, Joseph had been dismayed and tried to think of a solution to protect both he and Mary from scandal and contempt. But an angel had appeared to him in a dream and told him not to be afraid but to take Mary as his wife. That she would bear a son who was conceived of God so that the Scriptures might be fulfilled. Immediately, Joseph did as he was told.

The night Jesus was born, they were in Bethlehem. They had traveled for days to arrive in the city of their fathers to be counted in the census that was required of them. It had been a clear night with many stars lighting the sky. There had been no room for them in the inn, so Joseph found a small space among the animals so that Mary could be warm. Joseph was good to her, always looking for ways to make her more comfortable. Now as the time approached for her to give birth, she could see the concern on his face. She tried to reassure him that everything would be alright.

Finally, the moment arrived for mother and child to take their positions as life began its age-old performance. Other travelers that were close by immediately offered their assistance. The women scurried around, making preparations while Joseph and the other men waited in the next room. It was an easy birth; mother and baby came through the ordeal healthy but tired.

Mary had never seen a more beautiful baby. He was so small and soft. As she held him in her arms, he opened his eyes. It was a moment of bonding, mother and child, heart and soul. The words that the angel Gabriel spoke to her now came back as they had so many times before, "You shall call his name Jesus." How could this small fragile child be the Savior of the world? It was too big for Mary to comprehend as her infant child took hold of her finger, clasping it in his tiny hand. Maybe someday she would understand, but for now, she reveled in the moment of holding her baby close to her.

A few hours later, they received a visit from an unusual group of well-wishers. Some shepherds that had been pasturing their sheep in the nearby field came shouting and exclaiming that they had experienced a spiritual visit, declaring that the Savior of the world had been born. They were a boisterous group, praising and glorifying God, declaring that a multitude of angels had come to them announcing this great and wonderful news.

A few weeks later, Mary and Joseph took Jesus to the temple as it was the Jewish custom to dedicate him to the Lord and to offer up a sacrifice. They were met by two elderly people who prophesied and blessed them. Speaking of great things to come yet telling Mary that a sword would pierce her soul. She pondered all these things in her heart never fully understanding what all this meant.

Months went by and they received yet another visitation from an unlikely source. Wise men from the east had seen a strange phenomenon, a star, belonging only to a great king was seen in the heavens. They followed the star to Bethlehem to the child Jesus, bringing with them wonderful gifts to honor such a great king.

After they left, Joseph was warned by God in a dream to take his young family and flee to Egypt. King Herod had put out a decree to kill all the male infants of the region. It was a time of sorrow and anguish. A king gone mad while the blood of the innocents flowed through the streets. But Joseph, Mary, and Jesus had fled to Egypt where they were safe.

After two years, they returned to their home in Nazareth where they had more children and raised them with love and tranquility. Joseph had been a wonderful husband and father. He was a great provider as a carpenter, teaching his sons the family trade. He had been a God-fearing man and had instructed his children in the ways of the Lord. But a few years ago, he had passed away and left Mary and her children to continue the family business.

Now here she was, recalling the events of the past and not understanding why she was feeling so grieved.

Chapter 26

Later that evening, Mary enjoyed visiting with her sister, her children, and grandchildren. It was wonderful family time, and the prayers to Jehovah were heartfelt and sincere. James, Mary's other son, did the honor of reading from the Scriptures; and they sang worship songs in their Hebrew tongue, rejoicing in remembering the pilgrimage their fathers had made out of Egypt. But throughout the festivities, Mary's heart was troubled while thinking of her eldest son.

That night, as she lay in bed tossing and turning with no relief of sleep, her thoughts returned to Jesus. She hoped his Passover celebration had been a success. She was sure it was. After all, he was such a kind and gentle man, and his disciples loved him dearly. She smiled as she thought of Peter, James, and John, part of Jesus' inner circle. These were large, strong men yet so trustworthy and faithful to Jesus. Jesus always had a way with all of God's creatures. She remembered that as a child, birds would settle on his shoulders and crying babies would suddenly quiet down as Jesus tenderly stroked their delicate faces. She recalled one day watching as he squealed in delight while playing with rabbits and squirrels by the sycamore tree. Often, he would see her watching him, and a smile would light up his face. That smile that captivated her heart. He would run to her clutching in his small hand some wild-flowers he had picked for her. "Here, Mama, I picked these pretty flowers for you."

Mary would bend down to place a kiss on his chubby cheek. "Thank you, Jesus, I love you."

And he would respond, "I love you too, Mama." He would turn around and run back to his explorations of this wonderful world that he lived in.

Suddenly, a banging at her door disrupted her thoughts. Who could that be at this hour of the night? She got out of bed and cautiously opened the door to find John standing there. He was breathless and perspiring from running.

"John, what are you doing here? Where is Jesus?" she asked him.

"Mother Mary, you must come quickly. They've arrested the Master," he responded. Mary stood there stunned as the meaning of his words registered in her mind. Her knees became weak, and her head began to spin. John quickly reached out for her, but she immediately regained her composure. Jesus would want her to be strong. She recalled his words from earlier that afternoon, "Let not your heart be troubled." She quickly gathered her cloak from the hook by the door and followed John out into the dark night.

Chapter 27

Before arriving at the courtyard, Mary and John stopped to inform Mary Magdalene about Jesus' arrest. She quickly followed them outside, and the three of them hurried to the place where Jesus was being held.

Upon arriving at the scene, they found the crowd restless and wild. Jesus had his hands tied behind his back. His face was bloody and swollen, and his garment was torn, but he stood straight with a calm dignity. He immediately spotted Mary and her companions as they arrived. He looked at his mother with concern showing in his eyes. She was shocked to see what they had already done to him but was determined to stay strong for him.

As he stood in the middle of his accusers, Mary recalled another time long ago when he was only twelve. Some of these same religious leaders had surrounded Jesus as he asked questions and gave answers from the Scriptures. Now here they were, accusing him of meaningless lies. She knew that these accusations stemmed from fear and jealousy of these outlandish men.

Throughout the night, Mary witnessed the mocking and jeering of the crowd toward her beloved son. Occasionally, someone would approach him and slap him across the face. His nose began to bleed, and the bruises on his face became more evident. Mary silently prayed that this ordeal would end. But still, they questioned him and spit upon him. Finally, as the morning light filled the sky, someone suggested that they take him to the praetorium where Pilate, the governor, resided. They accused him before Pilate of forbidding to pay taxes to Caesar, but as Pilate questioned him, he informed the chief priests that he found no fault in Jesus. He then suggested that they take him to Herod who was also in Jerusalem at the time. But Herod and his men mocked and laughed at Jesus, sending him back to Pilate. Mary watched all of this from a distance. If only she could get close enough to comfort him, to touch him, to hold him. But the crowd was boisterous, and the Roman soldiers kept a careful watch on their prisoner.

As the morning wore on, Pilate suggested that since it was the Passover feast, he would release Jesus after a brief chastisement. But the crowd became infuriated and began to shout, "Release to us Barabbas." When Mary heard this, she was mortified. Barabbas was a well-known murderer! How could these people justify setting Barabbas free and keeping Jesus? The crowd became incensed and insistent on retaining Jesus. They began chanting, "Crucify him. Crucify him." They demanded from Pilate that he order Jesus to be crucified. At the word "crucify," Mary could bear this no longer. Great sobs of sorrow escaped from her heart. She began to try and make her way toward her son, but John held her back, fearing that if anyone recognized her as Jesus' mother, she would be arrested as well.

"Please let me go," she begged John. "I need to get my son." But John held onto her, holding her tightly in his arms, attempting to soothe and comfort her in her distraught state. This was all a mistake. Jesus was not a criminal! How could this be happening? Mary Magdalene began to weep silently, agonizing on what was happening to her precious son.

The Roman soldiers ushered Jesus to the open courtyard where they planned to scourge him with a whip that had pieces of metal attached to the end. John took Mary aside so that she would not witness what they were doing to Jesus. They could hear the whip lashing against his back while the Roman soldiers cursed and laughed at the pain they were inflicting upon Jesus. Mary listened to the lashing of her son while her heart broke at what they were imposing upon him, she sobbed in anguish. John held onto her while tears streamed down his face, and Mary Magdalene crouched down in agony.

When the lashing finally ceased, Jesus' body was torn flesh. He was drenched in blood and unrecognizable. Mary gasped when she saw him as they led him away to climb the long walk up the hill to Golgotha where the crucifixion was to take place. They made him carry his own cross across his torn, wounded back. Someone had placed a crown of thorns on his head, and the blood oozed out where the thorns had punctured his head. He was weak and barely able to walk. One of the Roman soldiers demanded that another man help Jesus carry the cross, fearing that Jesus would die before he made it to the top of the hill. The crowd of onlookers lined the path up the rocky hill. Mary, John, and Mary Magdalene hurried behind him, following as close as possible. Many of his followers sobbed as he passed them by, leaving a bloody trail behind him. It was a long way up, but he endured the climb up the hill just as he had endured the whipping, slapping, and mocking. He never said a word throughout the whole ordeal. Mary wondered if he was aware that she was there, but then he turned and looked at her with love in his eyes, making her understand that he loved her.

At the top of the hill, they laid him on top of the cross as they nailed the spikes into his wrist and feet. When they lifted the heavy cross up to place it into the ground, his body jerked as the pain surged throughout his being. Someone placed a sign above his head written in Greek, Hebrew, and Latin, "This is the King of the Jews." Mary, John, and Mary Magdalene huddled close together watching as Jesus hung between two criminals. The Roman soldiers cast lots for his garment as they laughed and ridiculed him as he hung on the cross. The chief priest stood nearby with his arms folded across his chest and his head held up with arrogant pride. Mary knelt on the rocky ground sobbing as she watched her beautiful son die. He did not deserve to die like this. He was a good man sent from God. She reached up to touch and kiss his bloodied feet where they were nailed to the cross. At that moment, Mary's sister came and knelt beside her. Putting her arm around Mary's shoulder, she pulled Mary close. Mary wearily laid her head upon the chest of her dear sister. Jesus seeing his mother in such sorrow, he looked at her with compassion and said, "Woman, behold, your son." Then turning his head towards John, he said, "Behold, your mother."

As Mary looked up at her son, she recalled the words of the old man at the temple when Jesus was dedicated as an infant. "A sword will pierce through your own soul."

Suddenly Jesus spoke out. "I thirst."

As the Roman soldier scrambled to dip a sponge in vinegar and give to Jesus, Mary recalled a happier time long ago when Jesus was thirsty. They were at a wedding feast and the wine had run out just as the feast was beginning. When she mentioned it to Jesus, he seemed to dismiss her concern; but having lived in the same house with him for so many years, she knew that there was never any lack when he was around. She informed the servants to do everything Jesus told them to do. Sure enough, he asked them to fill six water-pots with water. Then he told them to draw some out and give it to the master of the feast. When the master of the feast tasted the water, it had been turned to wine. He was delighted, for the wine he now drank was better than the first wine. How Mary had laughed. Only she, the servants, and Jesus knew where the wine had actually come from. Jesus always came through; he knew exactly what he was doing.

Now as she watched her son slowly give his life, she began to comprehend that this was the plan of God all along. She had been told by the angel that her son would be the Savior of the world. Today was the beginning of the Passover celebration, and he was the Passover lamb. As she bowed her head in anguish, recognizing that he was offering up his life in atonement for the sins of the world, she heard him exclaim, "It is finished, Father, into thy hands I commit my Spirit." Mary watched him bow his head as his Spirit left his body.

Chapter 28

After his body was taken down from the cross, Mary and the others followed to see where his body would be laid. They walked silently, each lost in their own thoughts, tears streaming down their faces. Mary's heart ached as she thought of the torture Jesus had endured, and the thought of him being gone was unbearable. But then she remembered the words he had spoken earlier to her, "My peace I give unto you." Suddenly, she felt a calmness come upon her. A comforting peace surrounded them as they walked toward the garden where Jesus' body would be laid. Mary knew that she had been blessed with a wonderful Son from heaven and someday she would see him again. She had enjoyed thirty-three years of his life here on earth. For that, she was eternally grateful.

After seeing the tomb, Mary, her sister, and Mary Magdalene returned to her sister's home to prepare the spices and oils for his body. They worked silently and methodically, anticipating the first day of the week when they would return to the tomb to anoint his body for burial.

The following day was the Sabbath, and as it was custom, it was a day of rest. But the next day, Mary and the other women left the house early in the morning while it was still dark. As they walked toward the tomb, they began to question how they would remove the stone from the entrance of the cave. Maybe they should have asked Peter, James, and John to assist them. But when they arrived, their worries were invalid, for the stone to the entrance was moved aside. Who could have moved the stone? And where were the guards that were guarding the tomb? As they entered the cave and their eyes adjusted to the darkness, Mary let out a small cry when she realized that Jesus' body was not there. Suddenly, two men in shining garments stood by them; the other women immediately became afraid, but Mary recognized them as angels. One of them spoke and said, "He is not here. He is risen!

Remember he told you that he would be delivered into the hands of sinful men and be crucified and the third day rise again. Go, tell his disciples and Peter that he is going before you to Galilee."

Mary stood there speechless. He was alive? He was no longer dead? She remembered him saying these things, but at the time, she was not able to comprehend what he meant. Now she understood. He was alive! She turned around and ran out of the tomb; she ran through the garden, over hills, and down pathways and, to the city, running until she felt her lungs would burst. She ran, laughing and crying all the way. People turned to watch as she passed them wondering why this woman was running and laughing throughout the city. She came to the corner of the street to the house where the disciples were staying. She ran up the stairs and burst through the door. She was breathless and excited to tell the wonderful news. The disciples sat there quietly, crying and grieving for Jesus. They turned to look at her as she exclaimed, "He's alive! The tomb is empty! He rose just like he said he would! Only we didn't understand the fullness of what he was trying to tell us."

"Oh, and Peter..." Mary said as she walked up to Peter, placing her hand on his shoulder. She knew that he was still feeling great remorse for having allowed fear to dictate his behavior at Jesus' hearing. "...the angel specifically said to let you know that you and the rest of us must go to Galilee and wait for him there."

Peter looked up at her with tears coming down his face and asked, "He said for me to go too?"

"Yes, Peter, he wants you there too," Mary replied.

The other disciples stared at her in disbelief. But Peter and John simultaneously got up and ran out to the tomb. Crying with her face lifted up toward heaven, Mary began to praise God and thank him for this miracle. She was going to see Jesus again real soon.

Chapter 29

Mary sat at the table with the rest of the disciples and their wives. They were full of unbelief but refrained from saying anything for fear of seeming disrespectful to the Lord's mother. One of the disciples gently tried to tell her that maybe she had imagined the angels because of the grief she was experiencing, but she adamantly denied it. She had seen the angels, and they had told her that Jesus was alive. Thomas, one of the disciples, quietly left the room. He was having difficulty hearing the mother of Jesus say these things. She was probably tired and distraught after the ordeal they had all been through. He decided to go out for a walk and think things over.

A few minutes later after Thomas had left, Mary Magdalene came running into the room. She too was breathless and animated.

"I've seen the Lord," she exclaimed. "He spoke to me. He's alive!"

Mary got up from the table and came over to Mary Magdalene and asked, "What did he say?"

Mary Magdalene responded, "He said that he is going to ascend to his Father and our Father but to go to Galilee and wait for him. But something else, he looks a little different. I didn't recognize him at first."

Mary pondered her words for a moment. This was all so overwhelming. She was anxious to leave to Galilee immediately, but the other disciples suggested she wait for Peter and John to return. It was still difficult for them to comprehend what exactly was going on. They had seen Jesus raise others from the dead, but how could he raise himself when he was dead?

At that moment, Peter and John entered the room. Every eye turned to look at them. They didn't say anything for several seconds and wore a solemn expression on their faces. But then, John began to laugh and say, "It's true. The tomb is empty!"

Everyone started talking at once. Mary Magdalene began to

recount to Peter and John that she had seen the Lord and what he had said.

Peter suggested that they keep the doors and windows locked, fearing that the religious leaders might accuse them of stealing the body of Jesus. James immediately stood up and began locking and shutting all the doors and windows. When they were once again sitting around the table, they began making plans to return to Galilee when suddenly, there was a change in the atmosphere—and there stood Jesus.

Chapter 30

"Peace to you! As the Father has sent me, I also send you." Everyone in the room stared at what they were witnessing. All the doors and windows were locked, but Jesus had appeared and stood in the middle of the room. Mary watched him as he stood there. Mary Magdalene was right, he looked different. His face was smooth. There was no evidence of a crucifixion on his face. Gone were the small lines around his eyes. His eyes were deeper, more penetrating, and his hair was a lighter color. Not only were the physical effects of the beatings and crucifixion gone, but his features were different somehow. He resembled the Jesus she knew, yet he was different.

He must have realized that they hardly recognized him because he then showed them the scars in his hands and side. With that, everyone knew it was Jesus. They gathered around him, each one embracing him. They began talking at once, delighted to see the Master. But Jesus walked over to Mary and, embraced her, then stepping back, he looked into her eyes and asked, "How are you?" She smiled with tears in her eyes.

"I'm doing much better now. Thank you." she replied.

He laughed and gave her another hug. "I love you," he told her. "You are a courageous woman. Have faith in God."

He then motioned for their attention and did something strange; he breathed on each of them and said, "Receive the Holy Spirit." And a wonderful presence filled the room as they all stood there basking in the glory that they were experiencing and praising God. With hands uplifted and tears flowing freely from their eyes, they gave thanks to their Father for Jesus and all he had done for them. When they opened their eyes, he was gone.

They stayed quiet for several minutes after Jesus left, thinking of all they had seen, heard, and felt. At that moment, Thomas walked into the room. He saw their expressions and wondered what was going on.

They excitedly began to share with Thomas that the Lord had visited them. But Thomas adamantly declared that it was probably someone impersonating the Lord and that unless he stuck his fingers into the print in his hands and side, he would not believe. He looked at Mary and put his head down. He felt guilty for not believing her story. He knew he was being stubborn, but he didn't want to get his hopes up if it was all a ploy by the religious leaders. Mary came over and placed her hand on his shoulder. "Thomas, we understand how difficult this has been. May the Lord reveal to you so that you may believe."

A few days later, they were once again in a locked room when Jesus suddenly appeared in the midst of them. This time, Thomas was present, and Jesus immediately approached him and said, "Reach your finger here and look at my hands. And reach your hand here and put it into my side. Do not be unbelieving, but believing."

Thomas immediately fell to his knees and cried, "My Lord and my God!"

Jesus answered him, "Thomas, because you have seen me, you have believed. Blessed are those who have not seen and yet have believed."

Chapter 31

It was a beautiful warm sunny day as Mary sat at the edge of the sea. The sky and water were a deep color blue, and birds flew over her head. Fishermen close by gathered their nets as they pulled in from a morning of fishing. The water was calm adding to the peace that surrounded her. She often came here to pray and ponder the things that were in her heart.

It had been an eventful month, starting with the crucifixion of Jesus and ending with his journey to heaven. She was grateful to God that she was present at his birth and witnessed his death, resurrection, and ascension. During the forty days that he was on earth after his resurrection, she was given the opportunity to see, touch, and speak with him. What a wonderful privilege she had been given.

Slowly, she opened up a small golden box that she held in her hands. It was one of the gifts that the wise men from the east had brought to Jesus many years ago. Inside were small mementos she had kept of her son. She pulled out a soft strand of brown curls she had cut from his hair when he was a baby. Next was a dried flower he had given her and the first pair of sandals he had worn as a child. She sat there gently fingering each item. She had loved him as her son, but she loved him even more as her Savior.

Many of his followers had enjoyed him for three years while he had been given to her for thirty-three years. He was in heaven now, and yet she always felt he was close to her. She talked to him throughout the day, not as her son but as her Lord and just like he promised, he spoke back to her. He had promised that he would never leave her or forsake her. She, for one, knew he always kept his promises.

He had commissioned them to spread the news of the gospel to the world. He told them to go and heal the sick, to cast out demons, and to baptize those who believe. Mary knew that she had her work cut out for her.

She was ready to do whatever she needed to do to accomplish the work of the Lord. Already, she and the disciples were gathering in different homes to pray and worship God.

Now as she sat at the edge of the water, she thought of all that she had been through from the day the angel Gabriel first appeared to her until now. It had been a time of heartbreak and a time of victory. If only Joseph had lived to experience all of this with her, but then the thought occurred to her: he must be with Jesus now. She laughed quietly, thinking how strange that her beautiful little boy that Joseph and she had raised was actually the Son of God. It was too awesome to comprehend but true, nonetheless.

Slowly, she placed all the items back into the box. She stood and looked out toward the sea, holding the golden box close to her heart. She squinted her eyes as she looked toward the gleaming sea feeling the wind blow against her and the warmth of the sun upon her face. She recalled how often Jesus would come here to teach the multitudes and heal the sick. For those who knew him, he was their Master, healer, Savior, and friend. But as she stood there at the edge of the water, she knew that she was the only one who could say, "My Son and my Savior." She looked up toward heaven with a soft smile on her face and gently touched her fingers to her lips. Then with a toss of her hand, toward heaven she called out, "I love you, Jesus!"

Bible References

1. At His Feet—Luke 10:38–42; Matthew 26:6–13; John 11:1–57; John 12:1–11
2. She Had No Right—Matthew 15:2–28; Mark 7:24–30
3. Who Touched Me?—Matthew 9:18–26; Mark 5:21–34; Luke 8:40–48
4. I Thirst—John 4:1–38
5. He Can Turn It Around—John 8:1–11
6. Mary—Luke 1:5, 2:51; Matthew 2:1–23; John 2:1–11
7. Crucifixion, Resurrection, and Ascension of Christ—Matthew 26:47, 28:16; Mark 14:43, 16:20; Luke 22:47, 24:53; John 18–21.

CPSIA information can be obtained
at www.ICGtesting.com
Printed in the USA
LVHW021032110820
662879LV00017B/655